PRIVATE
TUSCANY

First published in the United States of America in 1999 by

Rizzoli International Publications, Inc.

300 Park Avenue South

New York, NY 10010

Created by Co & Bear Productions (UK) Ltd.

Copyright © 1998 Co & Bear Productions Ltd.

Photographs copyright © 1998 Simon McBride

ISBN   0-8478-2178-1

LC   98-75132

Publisher *Beatrice Vincenzini*

Executive Director *David Shannon*

Editorial Director *Alexandra Black*

Art Director *David Mackintosh*

Stylist *Francesca Pisani Massamormile*

Project Coordinator *Emma Bini*

Publishing Assistant *Emma Head*

Printed and bound in Italy

PRIVATE
TUSCANY

Photography by
SIMON MCBRIDE
Written by
ELIZABETH HELMAN MINCHILLI

RIZZOLI
NEW YORK

CONTENTS

PREFACE

By Alexandra Black

Since the days of Imperial Rome, Tuscany has been regarded as an earthly paradise; a place of escape and regeneration, of rustic charm and classical culture. Indeed the ancient Romans set a trend for Tuscan country living that has continued almost uninterrupted over the intervening years.

Even when the main cities of Florence, Siena, Lucca and Pisa were flourishing through the Renaissance, it was the countryside beyond that beckoned. By the age of the European Grand Tour, Tuscany was well established as the most magical of destinations. Charles Dickens, for one, was smitten. 'Beyond the walls,' he wrote on leaving Florence, 'the whole sweet valley of the Arno, the convent at Fiesole, the Tower of Galilieo, Boccaccio's house, old villas and retreats; innumerable spots of interest, all glowing in a landscape of unsurpassing beauty steeped in the richest light; are spread before us.'

In this tranquil setting varied styles of living have evolved over the years, as these pages so vividly reveal. The farmhouse is the most simple form of Tuscan architecture. Originally little more than a bare one or two room dwelling, its thick walls were traditionally built from the field stone lying nearby and its roof covered with handmade terracotta tiles. When the land-holding system was rearranged in the 14th century, many of the farmhouses were vacated by their original peasant farmers and taken over by the middle classes who bought up land with their newfound wealth. They converted the basic farmhouse into a more comfortable place of residence but still retained its earthy quality, reflecting the pastoral traditions of Tuscany.

The same is true of the elegant villas, or *palazzi*, built by wealthy Tuscans since the 14th and 15th centuries. These beautiful homes combine the artistic sensibilities of the Renaissance with the rustic charm of the countryside. Symmetrical façades and refined

detailing around windows and doors are rendered in the local materials of stone, chestnut wood and terracotta. Loggias and terraces open on to pretty gardens replete with fountains and ponds, statues and marble benches.

On an even grander scale are the Baroque Tuscan *palazzi* with their exquisite frescoed interiors and vast pleasure gardens, or the fortress-villas that have evolved from ancient medieval towers into luxurious country residences. Both types of architecture survive, and now form beautiful homes for their fortunate owners.

In modern times, the inhabitants of Tuscany have brought a new aesthetic to bear on living in this idyllic corner of Italy. Where expensive formal antiques were once sought after, now it is simple farmhouse furniture of oak, chestnut or walnut that is prized. Bare stucco walls, terracotta floor tiles, and ceilings with organic oak beams provide the essential interior backdrop. These rustic textures and forms are combined with touches of contemporary luxury – swimming pools, underfloor heating, large picture windows and soft furnishings designed for lounging and comfort. And in the kitchen, bottles of oil and balsamic vinegar, jars of dried and preserved fruits and vegetables, almond biscuits, wild honey and wine from local vineyard form the basis of daily feasts.

Regardless of architectural style, the country residences of Tuscany share a common feature. They are conceived and arranged with the simple pleasures of rural life in mind: the views of gentle hills terraced with vineyards or orchards, the vistas of winding lanes lined with tall cypress trees; the changing light of the day from spring through winter, and the farming traditions that mark the passing of the seasons. Thus life in Tuscany is a self-contained existence, providing everything the body and spirit could desire.

OPPOSITE *The vineyards of Chianti are among Tuscany's sybaritic charms.*

ABOVE *A restored farmhouse near Cetona retains its original rustic doors.*

ARNO FIUME

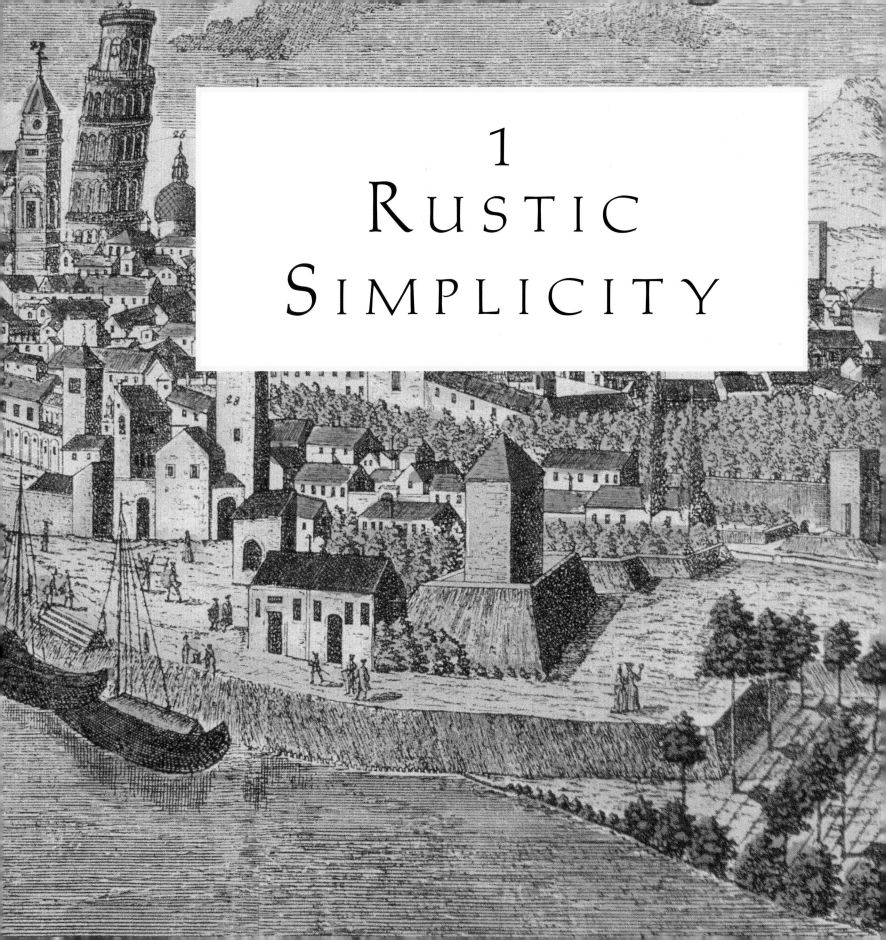

1
RUSTIC SIMPLICITY

PURE COUNTRY

ABOVE & OPPOSITE *The bathroom was originally part of the stairwell. The original steps still cut through one side of the room but now serve as shelves. Shiny tiles are banned from Ilaria Miani's houses – all is kept simple and rustic, including the mirror which is framed with dried flowers.*

ILARIA AND GIORGIO MIANI ARE DEDICATED TO THE POINT OF OBSESSION ABOUT RESTORING ABANDONED FARMHOUSES TO THEIR ORIGINAL RUSTIC SPLENDOUR.

It was while touring the winding dirt roads of the Val d'Orcia on their motorbike that the couple came across one of their most charming finds: a ruin of a house overgrown with blackberry thorns and ivy, perched on the edge of a plateau with breathtaking views of the valley below. The Mianis' passion for restoring farmhouses consumes all of their free time – they are always on the lookout for old properties to do up and live in for a while before moving on to the next one – and they knew exactly what they were getting themselves into. This was to be their fourth restoration and they relished the challenge of bringing the old house back to life.

The couple's projects always take their tone from the building itself, regardless of how little is left of it. A bit of coloured plaster still holding on to a crumbling wall, a small carved stone niche, a sagging painted shutter: these are the elements that reveal the soul of the house. In the end, when the work is done, it appears as if the house has always been there, resisting the passage of time yet wearing the years proudly.

The materials used in the construction are all rigorously authentic. The handmade terra-cotta tiles on the floors are from a neighbouring artisan who still lays them in the sun to bake them to a rich tone.

Roof tiles are moss-covered, culled from a nearby ruin. Even the wainscoting, painted by Ilaria Miani herself in bright, saturated colours, reflects local artistic traditions.

The landscape, too, is treated with the same reverence for the past. Obscured by jungle-like vegetation, the original vineyard and olive grove were uncovered and reinstated, and the old crumbling stone walls, used to terrace the sloping terrain, were carefully rebuilt. The original farmhouse grounds yielded a vegetable garden and a grape-covered arbour for outdoor meals. The only modern addition was the swimming pool, carefully hidden behind hedges and retaining walls.

It is only in the furnishing that comfort supersedes rusticity. Almost all of the pieces come from Ilaria Miani's atelier in Rome, where she sells exquisitely crafted reproductions of nineteenth-century furnishings. Small side tables, trays and book shelves cosy up to comfortably over-stuffed couches and chairs and romantically draped beds.

OPPOSITE & BELOW *The table and chairs in the kitchen look antique, but are actually creations from Ilaria Miani's atelier in Rome. Jars of paint pigment are displayed in a wall niche, originally used for storing food, while sheets of Sardinian bread, a handful of dried red chillis and a bottle of olive oil form an impromptu still life.*

LEFT *All the furnishings in the guest room were designed by Ilaria Miani and produced by local craftsmen. The original proportions of the rooms were respected, including the small windows, which frame picture-perfect landscapes.*

BELOW *The vast bed in the master suite is one of Ilaria Miani's newest creations and incorporates bands of rich colour into a bold design inspired by northern Italian furniture.*

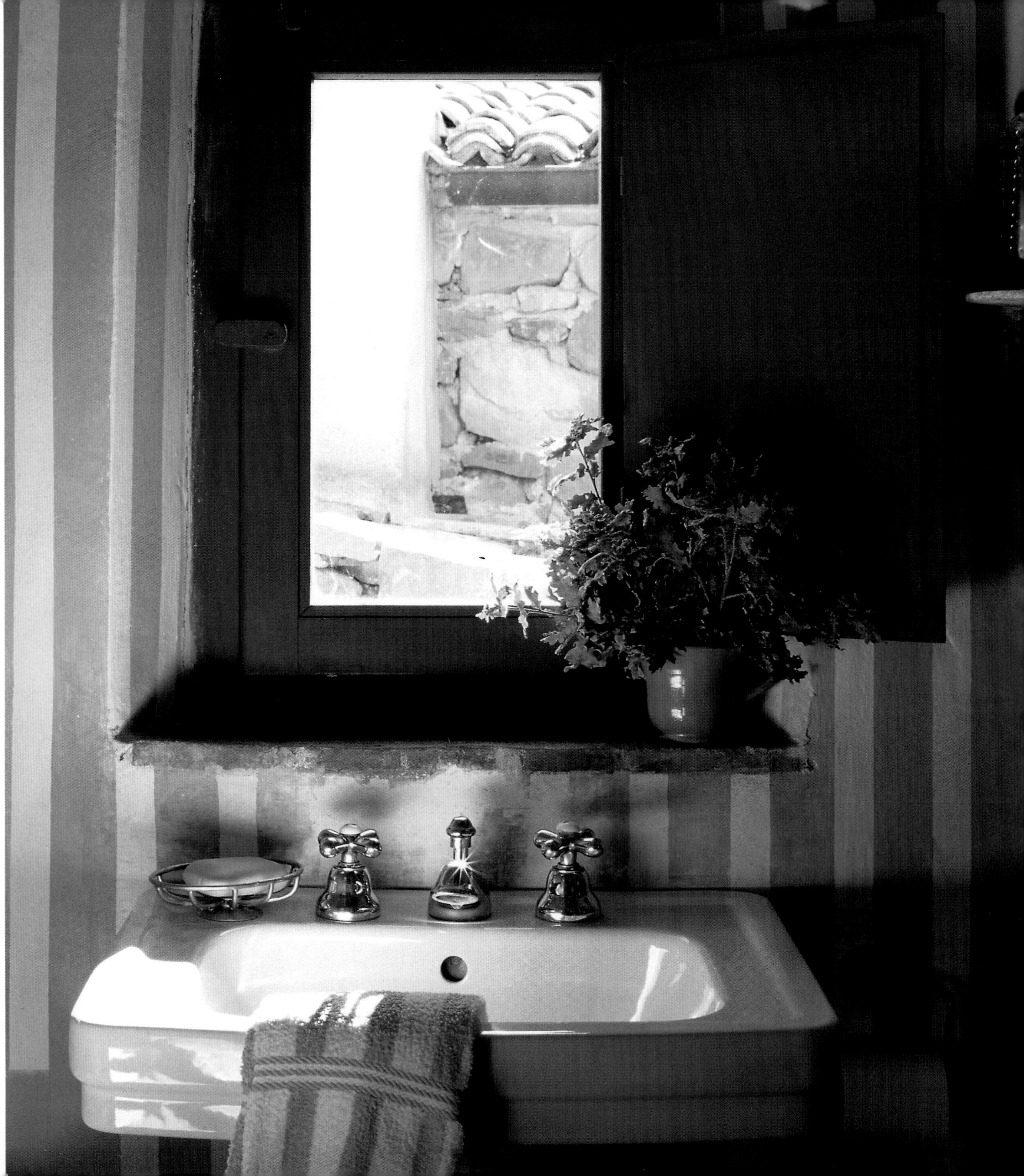

OPPOSITE *Sun pours through the windows of the upstairs bathroom, offering glimpses of the terra-cotta roof tiles and textured stone wall of the adjoining guest wing.*

LEFT *Folding deck chairs designed by Ilaria Miani sit in a sheltered corner of the garden, protected by a stand of tall cypress.*

LEFT *Grape vines that had been growing on the site for decades were coaxed over a trellis to create a rustic arbour shading an outdoor eating area.*

BELOW *The Mianis tried to leave the outside stonework as they found it. When crumbling walls necessitated some patching up, they mixed pigments into the cement to give it a patina of age.*

ABOVE & OPPOSITE *Delicate iron details reveal the owner's passion for the decorative arts, whether reflected in a spray of antique metal flowers in a simple tin jug or an elegant marble-topped console resting on a dainty base of painted iron tracery.*

CREATING ARCADIA

WHEN VITTORIA GRIFFONI WAS SEARCHING FOR A VACATION HOME IN THE TUSCAN COUNTRYSIDE AROUND FASHIONABLE CETONA, SHE NEVER ENVISIONED BUILDING ONE FROM SCRATCH.

It was only when a friend showed her a magnificent site, with a panoramic position and great stands of century-old oak trees, that Griffoni entertained thoughts of constructing her own villa on the empty plot. For the design of the house she turned to architect Cesare Rovati for help. He developed a home that, while not a slavish copy of a rustic farmhouse, takes all of its cues from Tuscan tradition. Hand-laid stone walls support terra-cotta-tiled roofs, using traditional materials to excellent effect. The rooms, however, are a far cry from the dark, low-ceilinged spaces that characterize many farmhouse interiors. Gracious proportions define the areas used for entertaining. The living room flows into the dining room, both lit by large windows taking in the view.

Outside, a portico with three graceful arches looks over the vast lawn, and in the two decades since the house was built vines and creepers have climbed their way over the house, making it appear part of the landscape in which it is set.

Griffoni has a special affinity with nature and fell in love with the enormous oak trees on the property. But it was not until the simple villa was completed that she thought about tidying up the grounds. At the house-warming party she threw, landscape architect Pietro Porcinai

ABOVE & OPPOSITE *Vittoria Griffoni's extensive collection of eighteenth- and nineteenth-century tin boxes appears throughout the house, decorating a narrow shelf above the staircase and forming clusters on side tables in the living room. The boxes are English antiques and were originally used to store tea or biscuits.*

mentioned to her that although the house had turned out splendidly, the surrounding trees were really its best feature. He gently turned Griffoni's attention to the garden, which she urged him to design for her.

A great sweep of lawn now leads down to a duck-filled pond. A wide selection of trees was planted near the house, to show off and contrast with the great oaks. Wide borders of flowering perennials still bear Porcinai's imprint. A newer formal garden was recently planted near the house with the help of designer Federico Forquet.

The interiors are a highly sophisticated reflection of their owner. Just as the structure of the house combines the charm of more traditional materials with the space and light of modern architectural sensibilities, so too the decoration of the rooms mixes old and new to great effect. Griffoni's unerring eye for antique furnishings has unearthed exquisitely carved and painted chests and armoires, which form the perfect counterpoint to the modern additions.

Comfortable couches and chairs, many covered in the antique needlepoint Griffoni collects, form intimate seating groups throughout the house. Griffoni is an avid collector of many things, both large and small. Her bronze and lead dogs, mostly English eighteenth- and nineteenth-century sculptures, are gathered in various rooms. Her vast assortment of antique English tea and biscuit boxes covers several tables.

Not only does Griffoni collect beautiful objects, she creates them as well. Her small-scale, three-dimensional wax collages depict fruits and vegetables gathered into woven baskets, combining her eye for decorative detail and her passion for nature. What began as little more than a hobby has now taken on a life of its own. These naive works are avidly collected, and can be found in the homes of such art aficionados as Franco Zeffirelli and Piero Tosi.

LEFT *This corner of the dining room is given over to an informal sitting area, centring on an open fireplace. It is purely decorative during the hot summer months, but during winter warms the room with a roaring fire in the hearth.*

BELOW *In the living room, luxury surfaces such as the discreet marble fireplace surround and the embroidered sofa provide the backdrop for rougher, more rustic elements such as the terra-cotta flagstones, a collection of antique tins and the stone intarsia panel above the fireplace.*

OPPOSITE & ABOVE

The master bedroom contains some of Vittoria Griffoni's most precious antiques, mostly dating from the sixteenth century and bought in Florence. The seventeenth-century wrought-iron bed is draped in a sheer white fabric, framing the magnificent view of cypresses, olive trees and the rolling hillsides of the Tuscan landscape beyond her window. Griffoni's passion for antique fabrics finds its natural expression in her bedroom. Here she has used some particularly beautiful pieces from her vast collection – the pelmet over the window is an antique petit-point rarity from Florence. The framed piece above the bed and the cushion covers are also antique textiles.

ABOVE & OPPOSITE

A charming country kitchen provides a focal point for household life. Unlike many Tuscan kitchens with their dark timbers and solid proportions, Griffoni's is bright and calming, with whites and creams the predominant colours. The ceiling beams have been picked out in a shade of vanilla to expand the sense of space and light, while bunches of dried herbs, braided onions and animal prints lend an earthy sensuality. The centrepiece of the room is a large wood-burning stove covered in delicately patterned tiles. Delicious home-made breads and pizzas, often incorporating local produce such as olives, fresh sage and tomatoes, are served around the kitchen table.

ABOVE & OPPOSITE *The house provides not only a studio for Tom Corey, but also display space for his large works. A corner of the sitting room is dominated by* La Casa Romana *from 1982. A pastel on paper, the work is based on sketches made by the artist in the countryside outside Rome.*

ARTIST IN RESIDENCE

OLD FARMHOUSES MAY APPEAR POETICALLY INVITING FROM A DISTANCE, WITH SMOKE CURLING LAZILY OUT OF THE CHIMNEY AND TANTALIZING AROMAS EMANATING FROM THE HEARTH.

The reality of this bucolic ideal, though, can be very different. Inside there is a constant struggle to keep out the cold draughts sweeping in under doors and through poorly glazed windows. So when artist Tom Corey and interior designer Adriano Magistretti bought an old country home, they knew they would have to make fundamental changes to incorporate all the comforts they had in mind. As Corey lives and works at the house year-round, the pair set about transforming the rambling old structure into a warm living space conducive to artistic endeavours.

Like many buildings that dot the Tuscan landscape, the house was actually a conglomeration of four houses, built up against one another and centred on the seventeenth-century tower which gives the house its name, Belvedere. The site, perched atop Mount Cetona, overlooking the dramatic sweep of the Val di Chiana, was also problematic. The zone is considered seismic, and so falls under a very strict set of building codes to guard against earthquake damage. Shoring up the foundations and walls with reinforced concrete, while still retaining the look and feel of an old farmhouse, made the project particularly complicated. Magistretti, who divides his time between his home in Rome, the country house in Tuscany, and travel abroad, turned his expert hand to resolving these

problems. He took advantage of the structural possibilities of reinforced concrete to create spaces not usually found in buildings of this type.

The living room, originally comprising four rooms (two up, two down), soars some twenty feet to create a towering, stone-lined room. Magistretti was able to tear down intervening walls and floors, yet retain the supporting stone structure, opening up the space while using the enormous new fireplace as a sort of buttress. The triple-insulated roof, stone walls and double-glazed windows make sure the house now stays snug even during deepest winter.

Corey's sun-drenched studio, with large French doors leading to the garden, is one the few new additions to the original structure. Here the artist translates his plein-air sketches on to canvas. His paintings, which are large-scale, almost abstract renditions of the surrounding country-side, are hung throughout the house. These bright splashes of colour compete with the real thing outside, making the Tuscan landscape a constant and essential element at Belvedere.

OPPOSITE *When Magistretti and Corey first bought the ruin of a house, there were four separate external staircases leading up to individual apartments. Dramatic restructuring resulted in a single residence.*

BELOW, LEFT & RIGHT *A sense of the landscape is always present – Corey feeds off its colours and light for his work.*

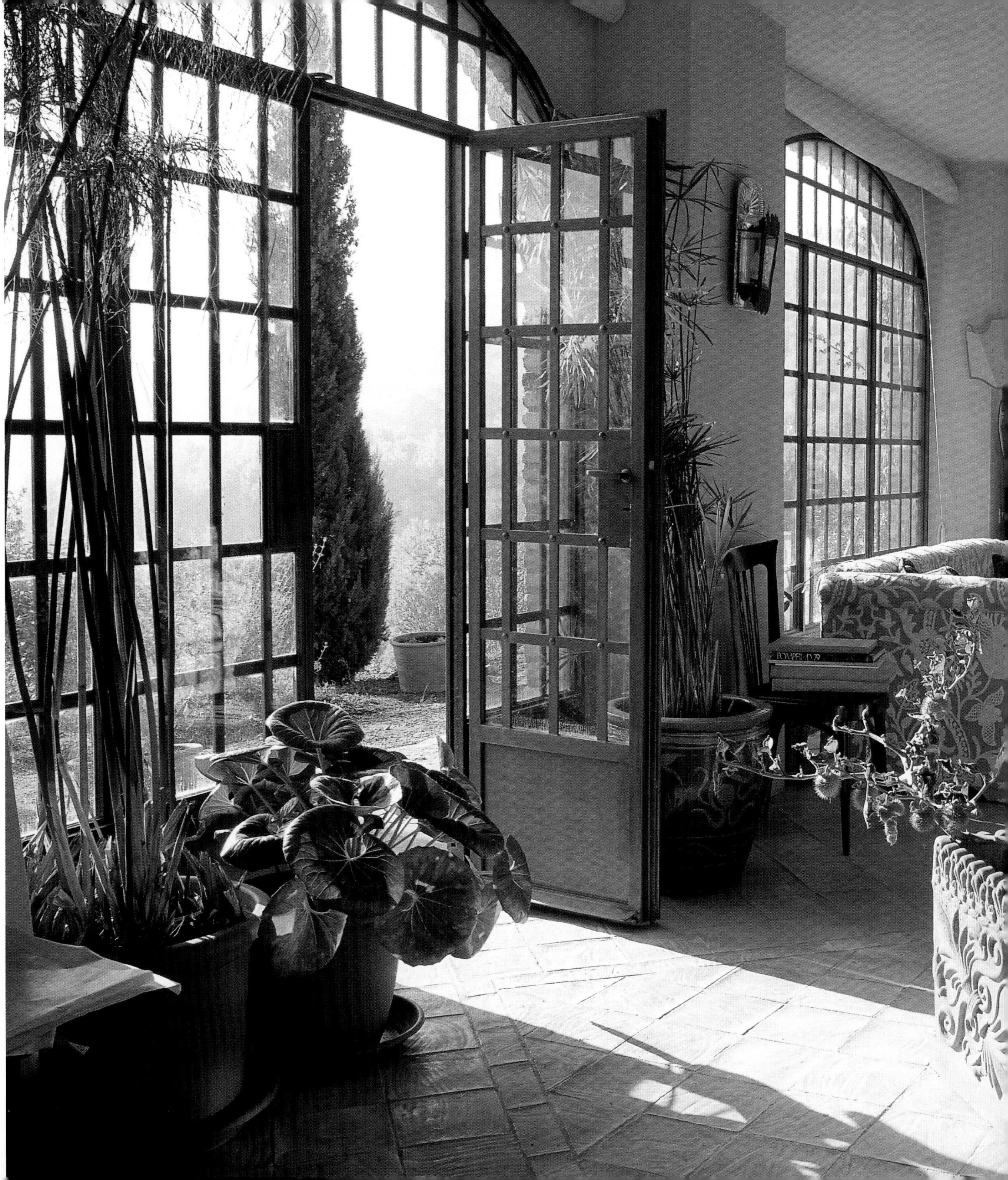

LEFT & BELOW *Corey's studio is a sun-drenched room that is part conservatory, part work space. Two of the four walls comprise wide arches filled with glazed panes. Not content with the views from here, Corey spends half his time in the field, capturing nature with a portable painting kit.*

BELOW & RIGHT *Dinner is served at a tile-
topped table, designed by Magistretti, while the
sun sets. The magical candlelit atmosphere is
enhanced by the wood-burning fireplace, used
to grill meats, vegetables and bruschetta – thick
slices of country bread dripping with olive oil.
The sunflower plates at each place setting are from
the Metropolitan Museum of Art in New York.*

ABOVE & OPPOSITE

The luxurious master bathroom picks up the warm ochre and yellow tones of the surrounding countryside. The room's colour scheme also bring to mind the earthy shades of Africa, an idea taken up by the tribal graphic on the vanity cupboards, and the use of dark, natural timbers. The overall effect brings to mind the dressing room of a Victorian gentleman in the colonies. Period details such as the light fittings and set of immaculate bone-handled grooming brushes add to the romantic mood. French doors open out on to a tiny balcony, with just enough space for a comfortable wicker chair. The view takes in the slopes of Mount Cetona.

OPPOSITE & ABOVE

A rich sense of colour, texture and pattern – verging on the baroque – defines Tom Corey's bedroom. The walls were painted by the artist in a sinuous design of yellow and ochre, which transforms itself in the ever-changing Tuscan light. A massive rustic Italian bed of hand-carved walnut forms the centrepiece of the *bedroom. The crown above the bed jokingly enhances its almost regal presence. The low, beamed ceiling and the terra-cotta-paved floor give the room a decidedly countrified aspect, which neatly counters the vibrant plums and golds of the bedcover and curtains. A selection of favourite prints adorns the walls and a treasured bear takes pride of place.*

PASTORAL SCENES

ABOVE & OPPOSITE *The warm tones of antique furnishings mark the living areas and provide the backdrop for refined touches such as the dainty piece of embroidered silk that is pinned to a cupboard door, or the silver tableware that stands on a magnificent bureau. This piece, a* studio mobile, *is from central Italy and is more sophisticated in design than most rustic country furniture.*

IN THE DRAMATIC COUNTRYSIDE OUTSIDE MONTEPULCIANO, A TWO-TIERED LOGGIA PROVIDES A FORMAL WELCOME TO THE HOUSE OF EMANUELA STRAMANA AND HUSBAND MICHELE CANTATORE.

The sixteenth-century forms of double arches are softened by exuberant Virginia Creeper, which climbs its way up and around the stonework. This imposing facade, however, is somewhat deceptive, as the home that Stramana and Cantatore have created is one of warmth and intimacy, a far cry from the strictures of Renaissance architecture.

Before moving to the country, the couple lived in a formal palace in the centre of Montepulciano. The building had once been home to the Medici family and was carefully restored to its former delicate beauty. But as much as they both loved the palazzo, Stramana and Cantatore felt the need for open spaces and so began the search for a new home. When they found Casteletto, perched high on a hill overlooking local vineyards, fields and farms, the simple villa was in fairly good shape, and they were able to keep renovations to a minimum, retaining the look and feel of the original structure.

A central courtyard, where animals used to be kept, now provides a focal point for the house. Although the building is quite large – there are seven bedrooms – a feeling of intimacy has been achieved by dividing the house into several smaller, independent suites. Cantatore, an architect who specializes in this type of restoration, converted the ground floor

ABOVE & OPPOSITE *The summer living room is actually a converted carriage house and is open along one side to catch cooling breezes. It is a popular spot for serving up easy summer suppers using straightforward Tuscan ingredients – Pecorino cheese, salami and plump ripe tomatoes – served with crusty white bread.*

into a large living room and connecting dining room. Antique terra-cotta tiles pave the floor and an immense fireplace occupies the far end of the room, providing heat for the entire space in the winter months.

The kitchen is Stramana's favourite part of the house. Its generous dimensions remind her of her childhood home, where family life revolved around the kitchen. It provided the setting for all the major household events, not just preparing meals. Indeed, stepping into Stramana's own kitchen is like stepping back in time. A worn oak table serves as a work surface, meeting point and supper place; copper pans and cooking utensils are hung on every available surface; and copious bunches of herbs dry from the rafters. Many of the plants are medicinal and are part of Stramana's research for a book she is writing on herbs and memory.

Stramana dedicated herself with equal enthusiasm to the decoration of the interiors, which are relaxed yet elegant and marked by an eclectic assortment of furniture. Some of the furnishings, like the master bed, have followed her from her home in Venice. Others have been acquired in Montepulciano or on frequent forays to other Tuscan towns. A common theme that runs through the house is her love of antique textiles. While many pieces were inherited from her grandmother and great-grandmother, others are the result of her continuous collecting.

The family lives here year-round. Once summer arrives, their life shifts from inviting fireplaces to the shady garden. A wide covered portico, originally built to house carriages and farm equipment, is now adapted to use as a summer living room. The garden is simple and Stramana's only intervention was the addition of her beloved herbs, which gently perfume the air on warm afternoons and balmy evenings.

LEFT *The kitchen, which was originally a store-room, is Stramana's favourite part of the house. Large, airy, and filled with an appealing clutter of saucepans and cooking implements, the room is scented by the dried herbs hanging from its arches.*

BELOW *Furnishings in the kitchen are all in the local style, sourced from second-hand shops and antique markets. They are notable for their sturdy, practical nature and comfortable proportions.*

RIGHT *The dining room is the most formal area of the house. Even so, the room is far from stuffy. The pristine white walls and lacy tablecloth are the counterpoint for simple antique furnishings. Bundles of herbs from the kitchen and racks of plates above the sideboard add relaxed touches.*

BELOW *Stramana's passion for antique textiles is evident throughout the house. Pieces from her collection appear in nearly every room, even if only a length of lace used to frame a window.*

OPPOSITE *A handsomely embroidered Arab wedding gown, a present from the brother of King Hussein of Jordan, decorates the entrance to the guest bedroom.*

THIS PAGE *In decorating the bedrooms, Stramana has paid great attention to even the smallest detail, whether a porcelain wash basin and jug or the antique linens and draperies enlivening a wrought-iron bed.*

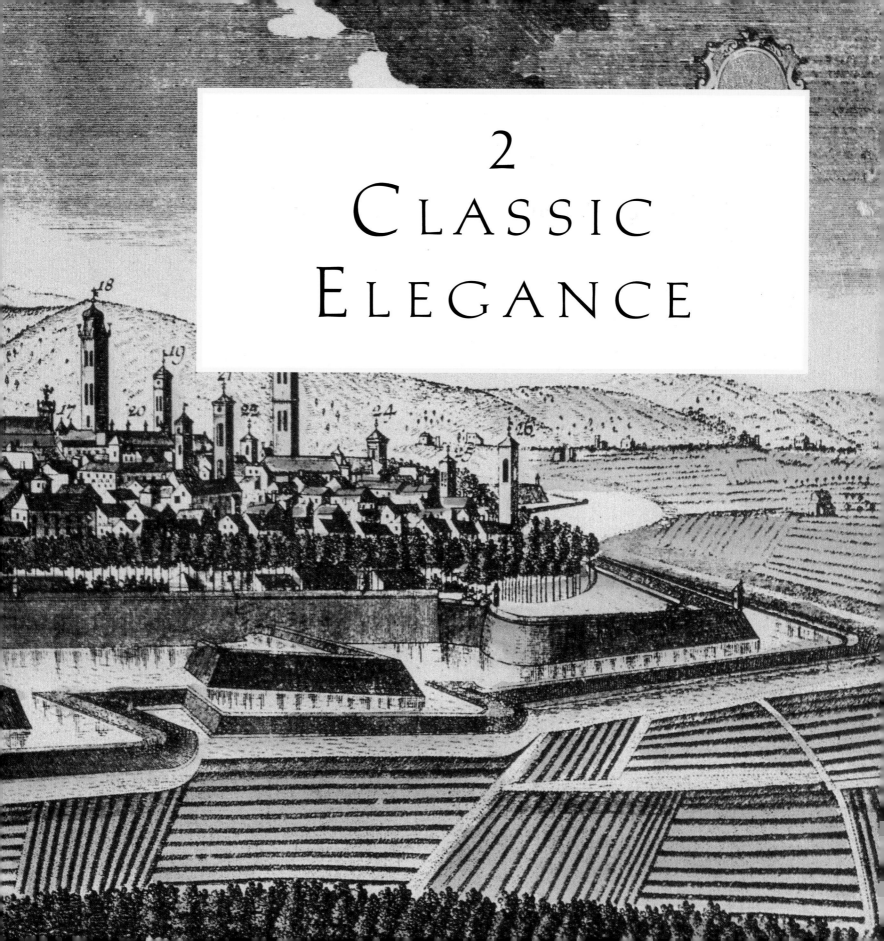

2
CLASSIC
ELEGANCE

ABOVE & OPPOSITE *Entering
Il Palazzo is like stepping back in time.
Generations of the same family have lived
here for centuries and evidence of their
presence is everywhere, from a treasured
toy steam engine – it once belonged to the
current owner's grandfather and now sits
atop a pile of antique, leather-bound books –
to a classic Empire chair, a family heirloom.*

TIMELESS
ENDEAVOUR

SINCE RENAISSANCE TIMES, THE VERDANT HILLS BETWEEN PISA
AND LUCCA HAVE OFFERED RESPITE FROM THE SUMMER HEAT. BUT
ONE HOME BOASTS ORIGINS THAT DATE TO THE MIDDLE AGES.

The foundations of Il Palazzo, a large country house belonging to an established Tuscan family, were probably laid during the thirteenth and fourteenth centuries, when the area was dotted with small, highly fortified towers, which formed a ring of protection for nearby Pisa. Most of these imposing fortresses crumbled over the years, but some served as the basis for later constructions.

The first addition to Il Palazzo is thought to have been made in the fifteenth century, when the land was handed to the all-powerful Medicis, who dominated Tuscan politics and arts. The gift was part of the dowry of Maria de' Medici, sister of Lorenzo. At this time the disparate buildings, including a crumbling tower and a house, were unified and turned into a hunting lodge. After passing into the hands of the Gaetani family, Il Palazzo was bought by the current owner's family, and has remained in their possession for the last four centuries. Unlike other homes in the area that serve primarily as holiday retreats, Il Palazzo is very much a permanent family base.

Although remodelled at the beginning of the nineteenth century, the house still retains the feel of a sixteenth-century country villa. While large in size, the rooms are on a human scale, and many still

ABOVE *An eighteenth-century wrought-iron bed in the master bedroom is draped in a sheer white cotton. In contrast to the romantic colours and patterns of the room, a portrait of the owner's great-grandmother is painted in the severe, dark tones favoured by English painters of the time.*

OPPOSITE *A long staircase leads from the ground floor to the main living area. Its spartan design is almost monastic in feel and harks back to the villa's medieval origins.*

boast the original terra-cotta paving as well as the massive oak beams that support the ceiling.

The ground floor has seen the most changes, due more to mother nature than to any of the inhabitants' tastes. The area is low-lying and years of flooding have necessitated raising the ground level several feet from its original location. This has made the ceilings on the ground floor much lower than they would have been in the sixteenth century, and some of the rooms are partly underground.

Another later addition is the loggia located at the front of the house. Although it provides a breezy terrace from which to view the surrounding walled garden, it was added at the beginning of this century and is in marked contrast to the modest tone of the rest of the building.

Despite the changes over the centuries, a strong sense of continuity runs through the home. In the garden, a large collection of exotic palms, put together by the owner's great-grandfather, still holds sway. Inside, many of the furnishings have remained in situ over the centuries. Some of the pieces bear witness to nearby Livorno's close ties to England. As a free port, Livorno was home to many English businesses and the trade in English furnishings was brisk.

Over the years, fine examples of this trade found their way into the villa, complementing its refined interior mood and adding a distinctive English sensibility. More recently, the current owner's wife, who is herself English, has added to Il Palazzo's interiors by bringing over many family heirlooms. These seem quite at home within the formal decorative scheme, their solid presence serving as a reminder of the villa's distinguished origins.

LEFT *The formal entry hall was tiled in a black and white checkerboard pattern at the beginning of the century and is one of the few rooms in the house that has not retained the original sixteenth-century terra-cotta tiles.*

BELOW *The restrained interior scheme is marked by the formal placement of furnishings and family heirlooms. In one of the sitting rooms, the bust of a family ancestor tops a grand piano.*

ABOVE & OPPOSITE *Handmade bricks pave the lushly planted dining area by the swimming pool. Palms and flowering shrubs give the setting an exotic feel. The terrace is a newer addition to the house and is used for summer lunches. The table is set with ceramic plates from Vietri.*

GARDEN PLEASURES

WHEN THE VINCENZINI FAMILY FIRST DISCOVERED VILLA AI SORBI IN THE HILLS BEYOND LUCCA, IT WAS IN A SADLY NEGLECTED STATE, HAVING LAIN ABANDONED FOR MORE THAN TWO CENTURIES.

Villa Ai Sorbi had been one of the most important properties in the area. Certainly the magnificent view out over the valley, unfolding from Lucca to Pisa, still reflected the commanding position of the once elegant and imposing villa. And the group of buildings themselves still held the promise of grandeur, hinting at the days when the villa, guest house, chapel and church formed the centrepiece of a highly productive working farm. The land, which stretched for miles around the dilapidated buildings, was as neglected as the structures – choked with brambles, blackberries and long-ignored grapevines and olive trees.

Seeing the restored villa and garden today, it is hard to believe that only twenty years have passed since the family began their restoration work. Life at Ai Sorbi revolves around the *sala centrale*, a typical Lucchese architectural feature. It is the central room on the *piano nobile*, or first floor, from which the rest of the house opens out. The room is reached by a double exterior staircase, its strong formal lines softened by pots of cascading geraniums.

Many of the interior walls of the villa have been decorated by one of the Vincenzini daughters, Ilaria. It was at Ai Sorbi that she first began to experiment in the art of mural decoration, from where it

ABOVE & BELOW *The villa's charm lies in its mix of casual and formal elements. An ancient staircase is softened by overflowing pots of brightly coloured geraniums, while the tiered steps of the terraced garden are edged with a profusion of trees, shrubs and flowers. The decorative garden includes the original grotto, now restored.*

OPPOSITE *The angular lines of the villa architecture provide the backdrop for a sweeping drive and a 1961 Triumph TR3.*

developed into a full-fledged career. For the portals in the main living room Ilaria chose the most delicate shades of grey to achieve a marbleized effect, which stands out from the pale peach-coloured walls executed in glazed stucco. Even the floor is painted in mosaic pattern, recapturing an eighteenth-century Venetian tradition.

Just as much effort went into restoring the grounds. The garden stretching up the hill behind the house, which included the ruins of a Roman-style seventeenth-century nymphaeum, was completely overgrown when work began. Today a pair of Tuscan terra-cotta figures stand guard over the rebuilt staircase leading up to the grotto. Old roses, jasmine and wisteria scent the air in this baroque corner of the garden. The area adjacent to the newly built swimming pool is completely different in design and is almost tropical in its luxurious overplanting. Bougainvillaeas and geraniums provide bold splashes of colour, framing the breathtaking view from the terrace.

OPPOSITE & BELOW *Rather than hang the bedroom windows with heavy curtains, Ilaria painted elaborate swags and architectural frames which embrace the windows without obstructing the views over the gardens and valley beyond.*

LEFT *The study is furnished in the Empire style, with bold stripy curtains adding a jolt of colour. The book-lined shelves contain both antique and contemporary volumes.*

RIGHT *Flashes of gold enliven the gentle pinks and creams of the* sala centrale, *the main living room. The angel is a sixteenth-century Tuscan find.*

OPPOSITE *In the formal dining room, one of the original fourteenth-century doors is marked by a cross, a reminder that the house was once a bishop's residence. Flanking the door are a pair of Queen Anne consoles dating from the late 1600s.*

ABOVE & OPPOSITE *Elegant sweeping archways and bright white walls merge with solid timber doors and stone-paved floors to create a balance of rough and smooth, refined and rustic. The entrance to the house sets the tone, with neat box plants in terra-cotta pots flanking the portico, which is paved in the large, unevenly hewn stones that flow throughout the house. The theme continues in the summer dining room, where large arched doorways open out directly on to the pool area and garden.*

RAREFIED ENCOUNTER

ONCE A YEAR, THE VAST, BRICK-PAVED MAIN SQUARE OF SIENA IS TRANSFORMED INTO THE TRACK FOR A WILD MEDIEVAL HORSE RACE, THE PALIO, IGNITING THE PASSIONS OF THE ENTIRE TOWN.

Although Paola Caovilla cannot claim to be Sienese, she has taken the ways of her adopted city to heart. She is an avid follower of the Palio, in which bareback riders compete for the honour of their neighbourhood or *contrada* in the highly charged three-minute competition. And, like the natives of her adopted city, she takes both race and surrounding festivities very seriously. Her villa, Fattoria di Mugnano, sits just outside the town's ancient walls, providing the setting for a celebration of the event which dominates the summer months. Caovilla decks the house with the banners of the *contrade* for the numerous parties she hosts, and serves dinner at a candlelit table, using specially made plates portraying the mascots of the race.

Caovilla and her husband, René, use the villa as a retreat from their home near Venice, where they design and produce jewel-like shoes for fashion designers Valentino, Ralph Lauren and John Galliano, among others. Enchanted by the beauty of the Tuscan countryside, its hilly terrain so different from the flat plains of their own Veneto, they acquired Fattoria di Mugnano some twenty-five years ago from good friends, who had lovingly tended the building for decades.

The Caovillas have changed very little of the house over the years.

ABOVE & OPPOSITE *Paola Caovilla's frequent dinner parties always feature her specially commissioned set of handpainted Palio plates, portraying the race's mascots. These include the double-headed eagle of the city's Aquila district; the oak tree and rhinoceros, representing the Selva district; and the dragon of the* Contrada del Drago.

The few alterations they have made include the renovation of the ground-floor section that was still being used for animal stalls when they moved in. It has now been transformed into Paola's summer domain: a large kitchen from where she orchestrates frequent soirées.

The couple's casual approach to entertaining is reflected in the way they have chosen to restructure this ground-floor area. Large slabs of irregularly shaped travertine – an element first used by landscape architect Pietro Porcinai in the garden he designed here in 1938 – were laid inside as well. The effect is of the garden and the house merging together, with friends and family able to move easily from swimming pool to living room to kitchen, wet feet presenting no problem.

The layout of the upper floor reflects the building's original use as a convent. Numerous bedrooms open off a long corridor, paved in a checkerboard pattern which dates from a 1930s restoration. The garden surrounding the house was also part of the same overhaul. The owners commissioned Porcinai, one of Italy's best-known landscape architects, to lay out a formal garden that mirrored the geometric facade and strong lines of the house. The rigid lines form the perfect frame for the rolling hillside beyond.

Coavilla decided to extend her connection to the land even further, and has turned the twenty-five hectares into a working farm, where she produces an exclusive line of products including wine, cheese, honey and oil. The label 'Ori di Toscana', or Tuscan Gold, reflects not just the rich hues and rare quality of the products, but the certain light that falls every evening over the hills, as the sun sets on Fattoria di Mugnano.

LEFT & BELOW *The large slabs of irregularly shaped stone covering the floor repeat a motif from the garden and provide a sturdy, fuss-free surface ideal for summer, when family and guests meander barefoot between the pool area and the house. Although the living room is mostly used in the summertime, a large fireplace keeps the house cosy during the winter months, as does a smaller fireplace in an upstairs sitting room.*

KINDRED SPIRITS

ITALY IS THE LAND OF THE EXTENDED FAMILY, WITH TWO OR MORE GENERATIONS OFTEN LIVING UNDER ONE ROOF – A TRADITION THAT SANDRA AND PIERA FONTANA HAVE TAKEN A STEP FURTHER.

When the two sisters from Florence fell in love with, and married, two brothers from the nearby city of Lucca, it seemed to them logical to set up house together in one big Lucchese villa. Each couple now has a separate portion of a large country house, which comprises the original sixteenth-century core and an extension that has evolved over the past few hundred years. Sandra and her husband, Luigi, occupy the oldest part of the building, which dates from around 1550. They have lovingly restored this section of the house, even retaining the original divisions between the rooms.

Their house-within-a-house is spread out over three floors, and an ancient set of wooden stairs still connects each of the levels. The kitchen and service areas are located, according to tradition, on the ground floor. The large kitchen was actually the only one in the original house and still retains its antique atmosphere.

The middle floor is dedicated to entertaining and contains the *sala centrale*, around which the rest of the house revolves, a focal point for family gatherings. Most of the rooms on this level feature decorative painting, a long-established interior tradition in the Lucca region, and a delicate border runs along the walls of the *sala centrale*.

ABOVE & BELOW RIGHT *Lighting is used to great effect in both the living room and entrance hall, enhancing the pale gold tones of the panelled walls. The two lamps marking the entrance to the living room are shaded with a typical Tuscan design, traditionally made from* pergamena, *a type of sheepskin prized for its transparency.*

OPPOSITE *A massive oak table stretches almost the full length of the dining room. A set of twelve matching chairs was a lucky find in an antique shop in Lucca.*

While the overall spirit of the home is Lucchese, the owners have avoided slavish adherence to any particular period or style. Sandra's passion for strong patterns, for example, is visible in the small sitting room on the first floor. Here, pink and white stripes envelop the entire space in a tent-like embrace. The furnishings are eclectic and include many family heirlooms.

Stripes are again used to bold effect in the garden. Handmade wrought-iron furnishings – a Tuscan speciality – are softened by plump red-and-white striped canvas cushions. Together they form an outdoor warm-weather sitting room, with a leafy canopy of trees for a roof and rows of potted camellias for walls.

The dining room was the most challenging to furnish. With a large extended clan to entertain, Sandra Fontana needed a large table. When she happened upon an eighteenth-century oak table in Florence, she knew it could seat the family brood with ease. A set of twelve antique chairs from Lucca provided the perfect partners, encircling its polished expanse.

OPPOSITE *The deep green of the park surrounding the house provides a luxuriant backdrop to the refined interiors, pervaded with a restrained Lucchese elegance.*

LEFT *A typical interior feature is the decorative treatment of cornices, skirtings and architraves. Here they have been given a subtle marble effect.*

ABOVE & OPPOSITE *The Fontanas acquired many of the furnishings from the previous owner as they seemed to fit the scale and mood of the interior spaces. In the living room, an enormous bookcase stretches almost the full length of one wall. It dates from the eighteenth century and was commissioned especially for the room.*

RURAL REFINEMENT

THE HOUSE THAT PIERA FONTANA HAS DIVIDED WITH HER SISTER HINTS AT ANOTHER SIDE OF LIVING IN THE HILLS ABOVE LUCCA, AN AREA BEST KNOWN FOR ITS FORMAL VILLAS AND GRAND GARDENS.

On the estates of major, and even minor, palaces, which served as summer retreats for the region's ruling nobility, there were always other buildings. Alongside farmhouses, stalls and hay barns stood the stately homes of the estate managers. The Fontana family lives in one such house, built upon and expanded over some four hundred years to create a rural abode with great warmth and character.

The villa is not immediately imposing, but slowly reveals itself. The building is immersed in a rich green park and is not visible at all from the road that passes nearby. A massive iron gate swings open to reveal a curving, tree-lined driveway which meanders through the grounds, finally arriving at the Fontana home.

The original nucleus of the building, occupied by Piera's sister Sandra, dates from around 1550 and is a symmetrically planned two-storey house, with a double exterior staircase leading to the central salon. Adjoining this formally planned facade is an assortment of rooms added on over the centuries, all surrounding a paved courtyard. The roof line undulates as each successive addition changes direction, giving the appearance of a small village. Interestingly, this sort of construction mirrors the typical style of the Lucchese village, in which the houses were

ABOVE & OPPOSITE *Avid collectors,*
the Fontanas display their passions through-
out their home. Antique silverware is
arranged on a console in the dining room,
while copper pots from Piera's childhood
home hang from hooks in the kitchen.
The huge kitchen was one of the few rooms
kept intact during the extensive renovation
of the house. The long wooden table and
cast-iron stove are typical of Lucchese
kitchens. The tiles are a modern addition.

built next to each other around a central courtyard.

It is this charismatic agglomeration that Piera and Antonio Fontana have lovingly transformed into their home. The couple took over the large and rambling villa in the mid-1970s, dividing the spacious quarters into three separate apartments: one for themselves; one for Sandra and her husband; and the remaining one for other family members. The Fontana family is not new to Lucca, however. For over a century it has been one of the biggest producers of the famed Lucchese olive oil, Filippo Berio, which is exported all over the world.

The Fontanas had a big job ahead of them when they began to work on the warren of interconnecting rooms that was to be their home. They took the tradition of nineteenth-century Lucchese villas as their decorative theme, and installed a delicate framework of stucco decorations to define each room. For the walls they chose strong colours, such as yellow and russet, for the sense of warmth and brightness they bring. The ground-floor rooms, for example, are washed in pale yellow, reflecting the light that floods in through the large French doors to lend the living area a soft golden glow.

Many of the antiques come from Piera's family, which is Florentine, but the majority of the pieces are reflections of the couple's passion for collecting eighteenth- and nineteenth-century Lucchese furnishings. Lucca has a well-known tradition of furniture-making and the couple takes full advantage of the local antiques shops, some of the best in Italy, as well as the monthly market in the main piazza, to search out interesting or unusual pieces to add to their home.

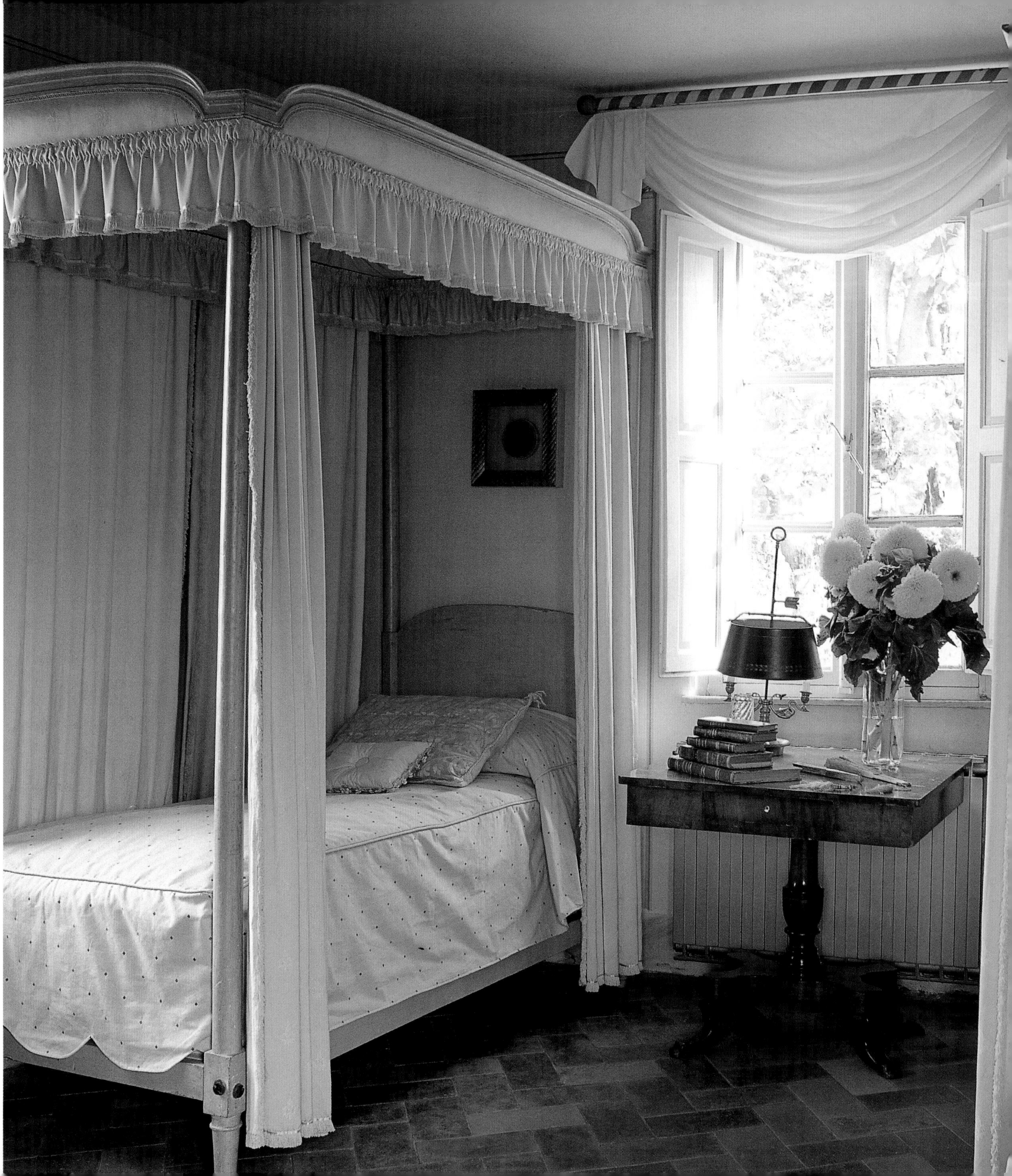

LEFT *A pair of beds, salvaged from a boarding school, are canopied and draped in a bright yellow silk that Piera chose to counter the lack of natural light in this part of the house.*

BELOW *Another distinctive touch from Piera is the use of chicken wire to face the linen cupboard she had built in the upstairs hallway.*

OPPOSITE *To enhance the sense of space and light, the original timber doors were replaced with large French doors which were fitted neatly into the arched entrance to give unhindered views out into a garden court-yard. In the hallway, a chaise longue from Piedmont in northern Italy faces an elegant Lucchese bench from the nineteenth century.*

ABOVE *A pair of eighteenth-century chairs helps form a conversation area in a small, sun-drenched sitting room, one of two salons on the ground floor paved in the original terra-cotta tiles. A large framed tax map, called a cabreo, also dates from the eighteenth century and is part of a collection of antique rural documents which decorates the room.*

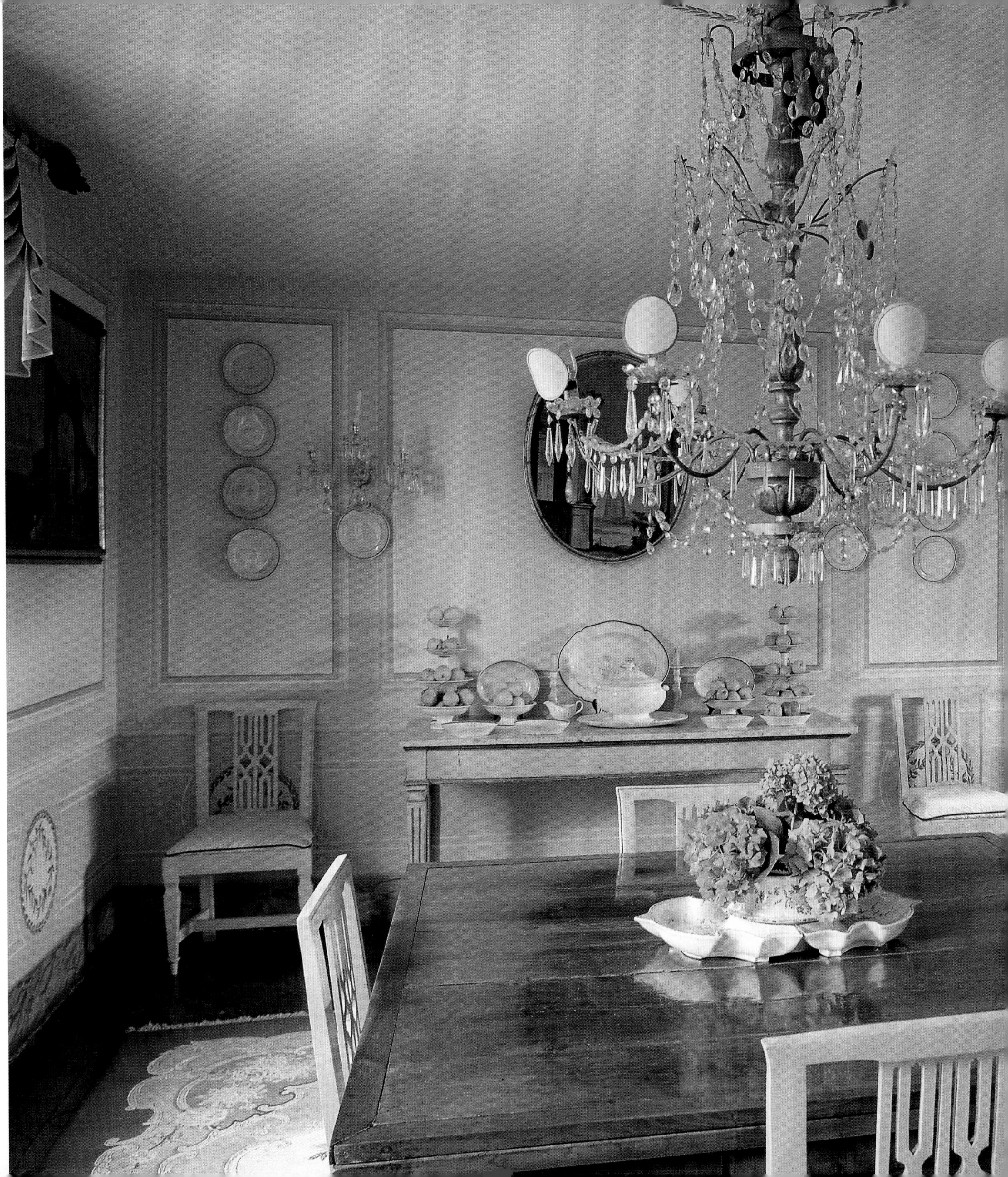

LEFT & BELOW *Lucchese elements define the Fontanas' dining room. The delicate trompe-l'oeil decoration and refined colour scheme are typical of the region's elegant style. Although the motifs and painting technique are originally Venetian, the look became especially fashionable in this part of Tuscany. Both the ceramics and a set of eighteenth-century chairs are from Lucca.*

ABOVE & OPPOSITE Don Guiso's love of the thespian world is reflected in the small theatre where he stages yearly productions for friends. His scenic sensibilities extend to the rest of the house. Even the kitchen sink appears full of dramatic possibilities when filled with an armful of freshly cut lilies.

STAGE SETTING

THE ENTRANCE GATE TO VILLA L'APPARITA BEARS AN INSCRIPTION BY TASSO: LOST IS ALL TIME THAT IS NOT SPENT IN LOVE. IT IS A THOUGHT THE VILLA'S OWNER HAS TAKEN INSTINCTIVELY TO HEART.

Don Giovanni Guiso's passionate love of the theatre and dramatic arts has become his life's work. It absorbs nearly all his time and is a recurring theme at his villa in the countryside near Siena, which is filled with books, objects and mementoes from the theatrical world. It is even equipped with a miniature theatre of its own.

While the spirit of the villa and its owner's life is easy to define, the architecture is something of an enigma. A striking formal facade presents the image of a grand villa, yet the rest of the house has the rusticated feel of a farmhouse. Intrigued by this apparent mismatch, Guiso explored the Sienese archives in search of an explanation.

The architect of the house was none other than Baldassare Peruzzi, the Sienese architect who made his name in Rome in the sixteenth century with the elegant Villa Farnesina. The double loggia of the facade was constructed as a freestanding pleasure pavilion, which was intended as a picturesque setting for outdoor parties. The house was added later, to give a practical use to this wonderful folly.

Guiso, the one-time mayor of Siena, continues to use his home as the setting for inspired entertaining, both inside and out. The garden, filled with fragrant lavender and broom, includes an open-air amphitheatre.

ABOVE & OPPOSITE *The dining room appears as something of a stage set, with its medieval-style decor, crested high-backed chairs, candelabra and symmetrical arrangement of objects. Two vases in the guise of Moorish heads flank the entrance.*

This exquisitely situated stage set, bordered by pedestals shouldering classical urns, was designed by the well-known landscape designer Pietro Porcinai. Dozens of benches line a semicircular slope facing the grass-covered 'stage', where the sounds of poetry readings and classical concerts fill the summer air.

The interior of the villa is equally inviting. It has been restored with a light hand in order to maintain the original forms. Spacious and airy, the lower level comprises a series of rooms connected by arched ceilings and massive pilasters. Piles of books, perched atop side tables, dot the living room, betraying the owner's studious inclinations. The dining room, almost monastic in its simplicity, is also on the ground floor.

Rooms on the upper level are designed for more intimate gatherings. Instead of the open, flowing spaces below, here the layout emphasizes seclusion and mystery, to dramatic effect. Bisecting the upstairs level is a long corridor lined with six wooden columns, each topped with a Corinthian capital. Many rooms open off this hall, imparting the feel of a convent cloister.

It is in one of these rooms that Guiso keeps his most precious possession: a collection of small theatres. Sourced from around the world, the stages come in all shapes and sizes. Used for puppet shows, they date from the eighteenth and nineteenth centuries. While the structures are authentic, the scenes they portray are the ingenious creation of Guiso himself. Working with such illustrious friends as Peter Hall of the Metropolitan Opera and Raffaele del Savio of the Teatro Comunale of Florence, he has painstakingly re-created small-scale productions of his favourite operas. On the first day of each year, Guiso invites a select group of his closest friends for a private New Year's performance, when the miniature cast of characters come to life under their owner's hands.

OPPOSITE *Don Guiso's collection of miniature theatres crowds the upstairs salon, some displayed on specially built plinths, others resting on antique tables.*

LEFT & BELOW *The ground floor is sparsely decorated, with heavy wooden furnishings establishing a solid presence in the large rooms. A seventeenth-century cassapanca, or trunk, in the living room is topped by a pair of Roman angels.*

RIGHT

Don Guiso puts his
collection of antique
tableware to good use
at the frequent dinner
parties he hosts.

OPPOSITE

The dining room
is architecturally
austere and minimal
in its decoration,
but it comes to life
in the evening when
bathed in candle-
light from antique
candelabra.

OPPOSITE & ABOVE

*Classical statuary and furniture from the
seventeenth and eighteenth centuries form a
tableaux in the upstairs salon, which opens
out to the loggia, or gallery. With its comfortable furnishings, white colour scheme and
leafy foliage, this secluded open-air spot offers
a restful place for morning coffee or for*

*relaxing with a book on hot afternoons. The
sixteenth-century double loggia is one of the
oldest parts of the house and was designed by
Baldassare Peruzzi. Loggias like this one were
characteristic devices of Renaissance architects, particularly in central Italy, where the
design of the open gallery created a cool yet
protected vantage point for admiring the view.*

ABOVE & OPPOSITE *Fattoria Mansi-Bernardini presents a sober facade, softened by thick patches of ivy and the shuttered French doors that allow sunlight to pour into the dining room. The dining table is laid with a set of antique dishes decorated with the emblem of nearby Segromino. The chairs, a wedding gift from Marchesa Mansi's father, feature the family crest.*

ARISTOCRATIC SECLUSION

THE NAME MANSI IS WELL KNOWN FOR ITS HISTORICAL ASSOCIATIONS. THE FAMILY WAS PART OF THE RULING OLIGARCHY THAT GOVERNED THE STATE OF LUCCA IN THE SEVENTEENTH CENTURY.

Today the most enduring reminder of the Mansi influence is the Villa Mansi, which served as the seat of this aristocratic family. The villa dates to the end of the sixteenth century, and its facade – a symphony of balustrades, loggias and marble statuary – is testament to the inspired intervention of eighteenth-century architect Giovan Francesco Giusti. His hand is also evident in the large romantic garden, which replaced an earlier seventeenth-century garden and wraps itself around the grand villa, now one of the principal tourist attractions in the area.

The Mansi family still owns the villa and Marchesa Laura Mansi called it home until ten years ago. But the family felt a responsibility to open the doors of this important local monument to the public and the inevitable presence of tour groups, art students and curious visitors would have made it a difficult place to live. So the marchesa decided to move to a smaller house on the property. It provided a more intimate environment, with the privacy and quiet she craved, yet it also had great sentimental value in its proximity to the ancestral home.

The Fattoria Mansi-Bernardini, where the marchesa now lives, is one of the *ville minori*, or minor villas, of the area. It was once the headquarters of the working farm connected to the larger villa down

ABOVE *Among the antique silver objects displayed on an inlaid console is an unusual collection of decorative shoes, from a full-size boot to a row of miniature slippers.*

OPPOSITE *The kitchen is a study in simplicity. Modern fittings sit unobtrusively under rugged ceiling beams and white-washed arches. Handmade tiles provide the pristine backdrop for food-themed prints as well as antique copper pots and pans.*

the hill. Marchesa Mansi had known the house since she was a child, as it had been given to her parents as a wedding gift by her grandfather in the 1920s. At that time the couple had set about turning the rather simple structure, which had been part of the working estate, into a comfortable house for themselves and, eventually, their children. Modern conveniences were installed and the entire villa given a contemporary look. The family used it mainly as a summer retreat.

A flower-lined driveway leads up to the Fattoria. The facade is sober, with the deep green ivy that clambers up the walls the only decoration. Opening out from the front of the house is a large terrace which gives views of the great sweep of valley below.

Upon taking up residence there in 1985, the marchesa redecorated the interiors, but retained most of the original 1920s floorplan. The rooms are artfully arranged, combining family heirlooms from the Villa Mansi with a house full of antiques the marchesa had acquired during time spent living in Venice. Chandeliers and sconces from the famed glass-makers of Murano throw light on her various collections. A selection of marble globes, from nearby Carrara, is arranged in the sitting room, while her collection of English Staffordshire porcelain dogs holds court from the mantelpiece in the living room.

While Marchesa Mansi no longer calls Villa Mansi home, the historic building, located just down the road from the Fattoria, is still very much a part of her life. She is fully committed to safeguarding and promoting this area of Tuscany, with its beautiful and rare villas. She is currently president of the *Associazione Ville Lucchesi*, an association that organizes visits to prized buildings, as well as promoting discussion of this living heritage through exhibitions and conferences.

LEFT *Groupings of treasured objects add a quirky touch to the elegant living room. Marchesa Mansi's collection of Staffordshire porcelain dogs holds court from the marble mantelpiece in the living room. The cluster includes a number of King Charles Spaniels, popular subjects of the famous British pottery as Queen Victoria owned one of the breed. A group of Venetian* mille fiori *paperweights occupies the central coffee table.*

BELOW *A pair of consoles support white marble globes from the nearby quarry of Carrara.*

Arns Fluui

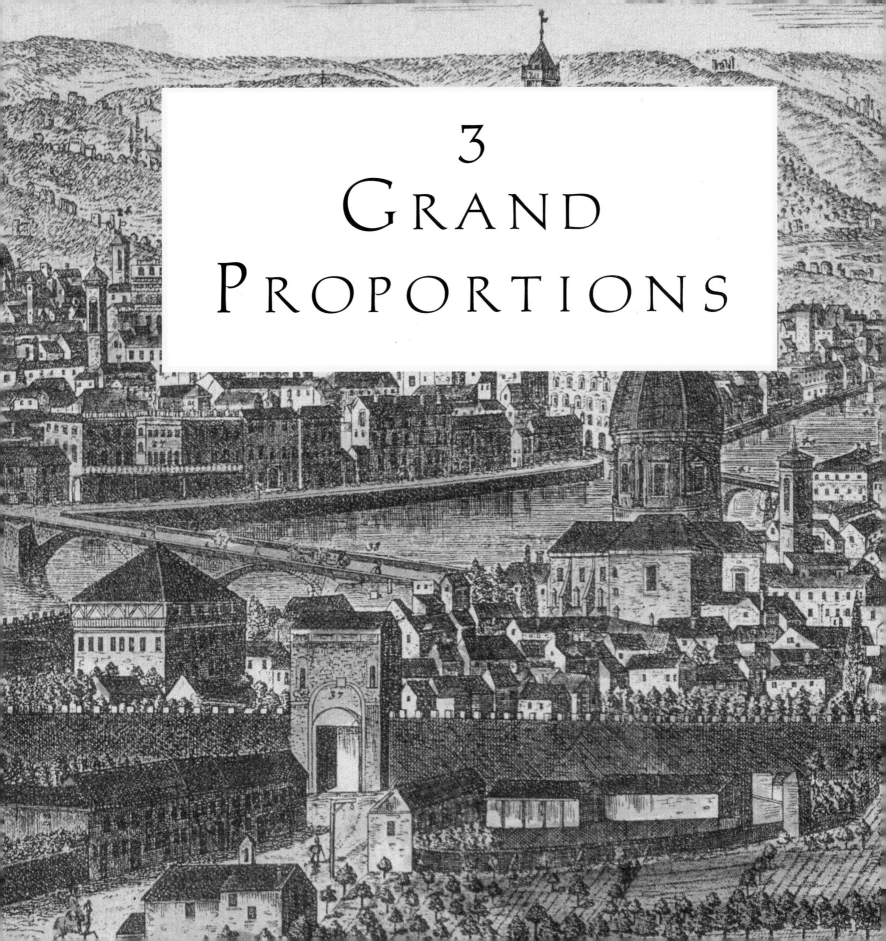

3
GRAND
PROPORTIONS

ABOVE & OPPOSITE *The facade of*
Villa Camigliano is a baroque symphony of
architectural carving and sculpture,
an aesthetic that continues throughout
the manicured grounds. In one of the oldest
sections of the garden, a seventeenth-
century statue is set into a rustic niche.

TUSCAN SPLENDOUR

OF THE MANY NOBLE RESIDENCES DOTTING THE HILLS AROUND LUCCA, ONE VILLA STANDS ALONE FOR BOTH ITS EXTRAVAGANT DECORATION AND ITS GENUINE SEVENTEENTH-CENTURY ORIGINS.

Villa Camigliano still belongs to the descendants of the man who transformed what was a simple sixteenth-century palace into the baroque fantasy that it is today. The original plan was square in design and dates from the mid-sixteenth century, when many villas were built in the area. However, when Niccolò Cesare Saltini acquired the property in 1651 he laid plans for turning the country dwelling into a sumptuous showplace. The double row of cypresses he planted to announce the villa's entrance still borders the dramatic seven-hundred-metre driveway. The facade was redesigned, incorporating arches and porticos covered with carved stucco and marble decorations, balustrades and sculpture. This vivacious mix of elements make the Villa Camigliano the strongest example of the baroque aesthetic in the area.

The owner, Saltini, had been ambassador to France, where he had been deeply impressed by the court at Versailles. Bringing back these aristocratic ideas to Lucca, he also extended his vision to the garden. While the villa itself remains unchanged, only parts of the formal garden, executed by French garden designer Le Nôtre, survive. One such part is the exquisite Giardino di Flora, which lies hidden behind large trees to the right of the villa. Two big fish ponds dominate the upper portion

THIS PAGE & OPPOSITE

The Giardino di Flora is ablaze with colour from early spring to late autumn. Interspersed among the flowerbeds are lemon trees growing in huge, centuries-old terra-cotta pots, hand-thrown and set with the family's coat of arms. Edging the garden is a marble balustrade topped with mythological figures.

of this terraced garden, while a balustrade topped with mythological statues frames the vista.

A staircase leads to a lower level, where a cool grotto, encrusted with stalactites, pebbles and mosaics, provides an escape from the summer sun. The adjoining walled garden originally hosted an array of exotic plants, the result of seventeenth-century Italian interest in all things botanical. It proved an enduring fascination, and in the mid-nineteenth century great examples of *Camellia japonica* were planted.

The estate still belongs to the same family, although the names have changed. In 1816 the last of the Saltinis, Vittoria, married Pietro Guadagni Torrigiani, who gave his name to the villa. More recently, in 1937, Simonetta Torrigiani married Don Carlo Colonna, Prince of Stigliano. Their descendants continue to call this sumptuous residence home but prefer to use its poetic title, Villa Camigliano, after the vibrant camellias that still bloom in the gardens each spring.

THESE PAGES

By the seventeenth century, grottoes were a common feature of Tuscan gardens. This splendid example is paved with a mosaic of riverbed pebbles and encrusted with exotic stones and statuary.

LEFT & BELOW *Baroque elements –*
such as the masterfully designed formal staircase
that leads down to the Giardino di Flora, or the
ghoulish stone water spout – impress at every
turn. Tucked away to one side of the staircase
landing is a small grotto which, like the larger,
more elaborate grotto on the other side of the
grounds, would have provided the original villa
residents with a cool refuge during the summer.

OPPOSITE & ABOVE

The main salon in the villa displays a rare unity in its interior scheme, painting and furnishings. This is because almost all of the elements of the room date from the seventeenth century and were conceived as a whole. Despite the exuberant surface decoration, the room still manages to maintain great dignity and elegance, thanks in part to the choice of colours – soft golds and pale porcelain blues highlight the ivory walls without overpowering them. The salon's symmetry, with each side of the room a mirror reflection of the other, also works to achieve an overall feeling of harmony. Windows are intentionally left free of drapery to maximize the natural light.

ABOVE & OPPOSITE *The facade of Villa I Cotrozzi is best appreciated from the formal garden, which stretches from the house towards the hills beyond. Wisteria and roses form shady arbours, and garden goddesses peer from amidst leafy hedges.*

ELYSIUM VISTAS

WITH A BACKDROP OF MOUNTAIN SCENERY, A HEAVENLY GARDEN AND GILT-EDGED INTERIORS, VILLA I COTROZZI IS A STUDY IN AESTHETIC REFINEMENT, A PERFECT EXAMPLE OF A LUCCHESE VILLA.

Originally built in the seventeenth century by a cardinal, the soft pink facade with green shuttered windows presents a rational and symmetrical entrance. The house was expanded and reworked in the nineteenth century and the current owners, the Petris, have tried as much as possible to restore it to its original seventeenth-century splendour.

Rosita Petri has taken I Cotrozzi to heart and has devoted much time and effort to perfecting its interiors. A lover of beautiful objects, Petri has eclectic taste but everything she uses is of the highest quality. The entrance hall, in typical Lucchese fashion, cuts right through the house from front to back, with the other rooms opening out from this. Black and white checkerboard tiles create a smooth, shiny foundation for the heavy petit-point rug that lines the hall. The furnishings here are rigorously seventeenth- and eighteenth-century. The central table, which always bears a massive floral arrangement, is First Empire. The divan and chairs, upholstered in golden silk, date from 1750.

Yellow also dominates the formal sitting room. Walls, curtains and couches are all covered in a bright yellow silk, providing an impression of sunlight on even the darkest days. The large room occupies an entire corner of the house. A pair of crystal chandeliers illuminate the space in

ABOVE *A row of terra-cotta finials marks the boundaries of the lush walled garden that flanks the* limonaia.

OPPOSITE *Rows of cypresses and broad gravel paths lead from the house to the garden behind. An iron balustrade, punctuated by stone pilasters and urns of pink geraniums, rings a water reserve.*

a grand manner, in keeping with the room's gracious proportions. Petri has, however, managed to retain an intimate feeling by creating two distinct seating areas within the large room. Antique Oriental carpets are laid down over a rich red carpet, further enhancing the warmth and cosiness of this otherwise formal environment.

The dining room is one of the few parts of the house to retain the original flooring – antique terra-cotta tiles. Using this tone as a starting point, Petri chose a terra-cotta red for the walls, which serves to highlight the Compagnie des Indes plates which hang there. A pair of eighteenth-century statuettes in the shape of turbaned Moors have been transformed into lamps and hold court across the table.

While the ground floor is mostly dedicated to entertaining, one corner suite is given over to a perfectly decorated bedroom, which belonged to the couple's daughter before her marriage. Rosy-pink draperies and bed curtains play off the moss green used elsewhere in the room. The top floor, reached by a modest staircase, is given over to the family's private quarters.

Outside, the villa's physical environment is more than a match for its elegant interior. Set midway up one of the hills that rise from the plain of Lucca, the villa is dramatically positioned within a garden that rises towards the mountains. One of the highlights of the garden is the ancient *limonaia*, or lemon house. While Lucchese winters are not particularly harsh, they are too cold for citrus fruits to survive. Glazed lemon houses were used to store the large lemon trees that, during the warmer months, were placed throughout the garden in their handmade terra-cotta pots. Although today the *limonaia* is used for storage, the balustrade which surrounds this outbuilding still bears the original terra-cotta finials, testament to an auspicious past.

RIGHT *Rosy pinks define this corner bedroom. The nineteenth-century bed is covered with a rare piece of antique lace.*

BELOW, LEFT & RIGHT *Chilean maté pots shine in one corner of the main salon; a Louis-Philippe crystal candelabra in another.*

OPPOSITE *The tiled floor of the entry hall is covered with a petit-point carpet. The Louis XIV console dates from circa 1600.*

LEFT *The dining-room walls are hung with a collection of Ginori plates in the Tulipano pattern, dating from around 1700. The pair of statues, converted into lamps, is also eighteenth-century.*

BELOW *A corridor stretches the length of the house, its walls painted with trompe-l'oeil panels and the ceiling with trompe-l'oeil roundels.*

ABOVE & OPPOSITE *The vivid surface decoration of the villa interiors has been faithfully preserved. Sometimes this decoration takes the form of frescoes painted directly on to the stucco walls, as in the entrance to the main salon, which is framed by fanciful trelliswork. Other surfaces are covered in* papier peint, *a handpainted wallpaper imported from France at the turn of the century, depicting idyllic country scenes.*

RENAISSANCE FABLE

A FEW MILES FROM CORTONA, THE SUMPTUOUS RENAISSANCE VILLA OF SILVIO AND SIMONE PASSERINI, REPLETE WITH WALL AND CEILING FRESCOES, BELIES ITS HUMBLE FARMHOUSE ORIGINS.

The oldest elements within the Passerini villa date back to the sixteenth century, when it most likely started out as a simple farmhouse. Yet centuries of change have turned it into an imposing frescoed villa complete with a formal, enclosed garden. The villa was owned by the Mancini family until the middle of the last century. A marriage to the Passerini clan changed its name, but kept it in the same family.

The approach to the villa passes by one of its most striking features: a walled reservoir, now used as a swimming pool during the hot summer months. A small stone bridge links the grassy island in the centre to the 'mainland'. The little islet is shaded by a centuries-old and rare pepper tree. A constant flow of water from a nearby spring keeps the pool fresh and cool.

The interiors are formal and bear the traces of generations of Mancinis and Passerinis. A long corridor which bisects the main wing of the house is covered in *papier peint*, a handpainted wallpaper imported from France around the turn of the century. The landscapes decorating the living room date from the beginning of the nineteenth century. Depicting bucolic settings with lakes, hills and villas, the soft green tones rival the views from the window to the surrounding countryside.

ABOVE & OPPOSITE *The upstairs hallway is covered in panels of handpainted wallpaper featuring idealized landscapes. In the main salon a trompe-l'oeil detail contrasts with heavy, natural oak doors .*

RIGHT *The rough and refined meet again in the form of a handsomely carved chair, hung with horse bridle, and an antique glazed terra-cotta urn once used to store oil.*

A chapel behind the house dates from the eighteenth century, but it was decorated later, around 1800. The trompe-l'oeil facade, which gives the rather simple entrance a peaked roof and bell tower, presides over the inner courtyard. A *limonaia* faces the main gate, its interiors a mix of frescoes from the eighteenth and nineteenth century. The swags and geometrical decorations, along with troops of rigidly posed Napoleonic soldiers, playfully recall the French occupation of Italy. Rows of lemon trees in hand-thrown terra-cotta urns are carried from the garden to this light-filled room to winter over the cold months.

The formal garden is enclosed on all four sides by a high wall, pierced by a fanciful eighteenth-century gateway. Box hedges divide the parterres and a collection of rare camellias provides colour. The camellias, probably planted in the nineteenth century, have thrived in the microclimate provided by the high walls and the large magnolia tree, shading these delicate plants from the blistering heat of summer.

OPPOSITE & THIS PAGE *The main salon was frescoed at the beginning of the nineteenth century and depicts landscapes set with large shimmering lakes. Classical columns are intended to create the illusion that a loggia wraps around the room, providing views of a perfect countryside, complete with birds flying overhead.*

OPPOSITE
A walled garden provides the prefect microclimate for growing a collection of rare camellias, very unusual for this part of Tuscany.

LEFT
The chapel entrance is marked with the trompe-l'oeil image of a church.

LEFT & BELOW *A stone reservoir in the garden dates from the nineteenth century and is used today as a swimming pond. A small island, shaded by an ancient pepper tree and furnished with sun loungers, is reached by a stone bridge.*

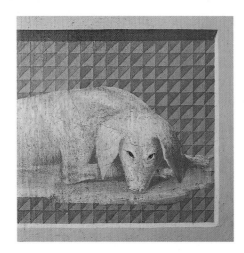

ABOVE & OPPOSITE *Nineteenth-century frescoes in pastel shades define the ground-floor salons. Although much of this decoration is purely stylistic, the portrait of a greyhound, symbolic of fidelity, appears beneath a window in the living room.*

NOBLE REPUTATION

EACH SUMMER, THE APPROACH TO THIS VILLA JUST OUTSIDE CORTONA IS FLANKED BY FIELDS OF BRIGHT SUNFLOWERS AND RIPE BROWN WHEAT, INTERWOVEN WITH EMERALD-GREEN VINEYARDS.

Abruptly the rustic feeling gives way to a more formal establishment: the *villa padronale*, literally 'the owner's villa'. Traditionally the seat of the man who owned and oversaw production on the land, this historically intriguing villa is no exception. The owner, who restored the villa to its original splendour in 1980, is very much involved in the day-to-day business of running a sizeable agricultural venture.

Although the villa had been in his family's hands for generations, by the time the current owner decided to take up residence in the late 1970s it was in a sorry state. Damaged during the Second World War, the building had been abandoned and subsequently left to crumble. After several years of painstaking restoration, the owner and his family moved in, furnishing their new home with family heirlooms as well as newly acquired antiques.

The villa's unique character stems from the fact that it was built and added to over a period of three hundred years. The architectural and decorative details all bear witness to three distinctive periods: the seventeenth, eighteenth and nineteenth centuries.

The dining room is located in the oldest section of the villa, which dates from the seventeenth century. Marvellous naive frescoes, obscured

ABOVE & OPPOSITE *During the restoration of the house in the late 1970s the villa was brought up to date. Here, a bathroom was fashioned from an ingeniously frescoed room featuring garden scenes, a delicate balustrade and a canopied tent.*

by thick layers of paint, were lovingly uncovered by the present owners and restored to their former beauty. Enchanting animal portraits now provide a charming backdrop to the set of eighteenth-century Lucchese chairs which surround the dining table.

The main salon is located in a newer part of the villa and the decoration bears the date 1804. A domed, coffered ceiling painted in traditional two-tone *faux* grisaille, looms above the large room. Peach-coloured panels host a collection of family portraits, while portraits of another sort, a pair of greyhounds, appear as frescoes under the two large windows. Such universal symbols of fidelity were a common theme in the grand houses around Cortona.

Many of the rooms still bear the original fresco decorations. The walls of the master bedroom feature an elaborate painted doorframe, although the doorway is no longer functional. A bathroom has been carved out of a room ingeniously decorated in the nineteenth century with a balustrade offering views of an idealized countryside. A *faux* tent canopy provides the finishing touch to this magical room.

While the presence of so much fresco decoration has an immediate and sometimes theatrical impact, the more subtle elements of the structure are just as charming. Original terra-cotta floors pave most of the villa and carved details of local *pietra serena* stone, such as corbels, steps and windowsills, lend a sense of permanence and place.

A formal garden surrounds the villa, giving way to a less well-tended area that the owner refers to as 'sauvage'. This, in turn, adjoins some hundred hectares of land which continue to be worked, year after year, oblivious to the changing fortunes of the villa perched above.

OPPOSITE & LEFT Pietra serena, *a grey stone, and warm terra-cotta tiles are typical Tuscan building elements that appear throughout the villa. A corbel carved of* pietra serena *provides support for the soaring arches in the entrance.*

BELOW *The main salon retains its original nineteenth-century grisaille decoration, but large, comfortable sofas and leafy pot plants help to create a more relaxed environment.*

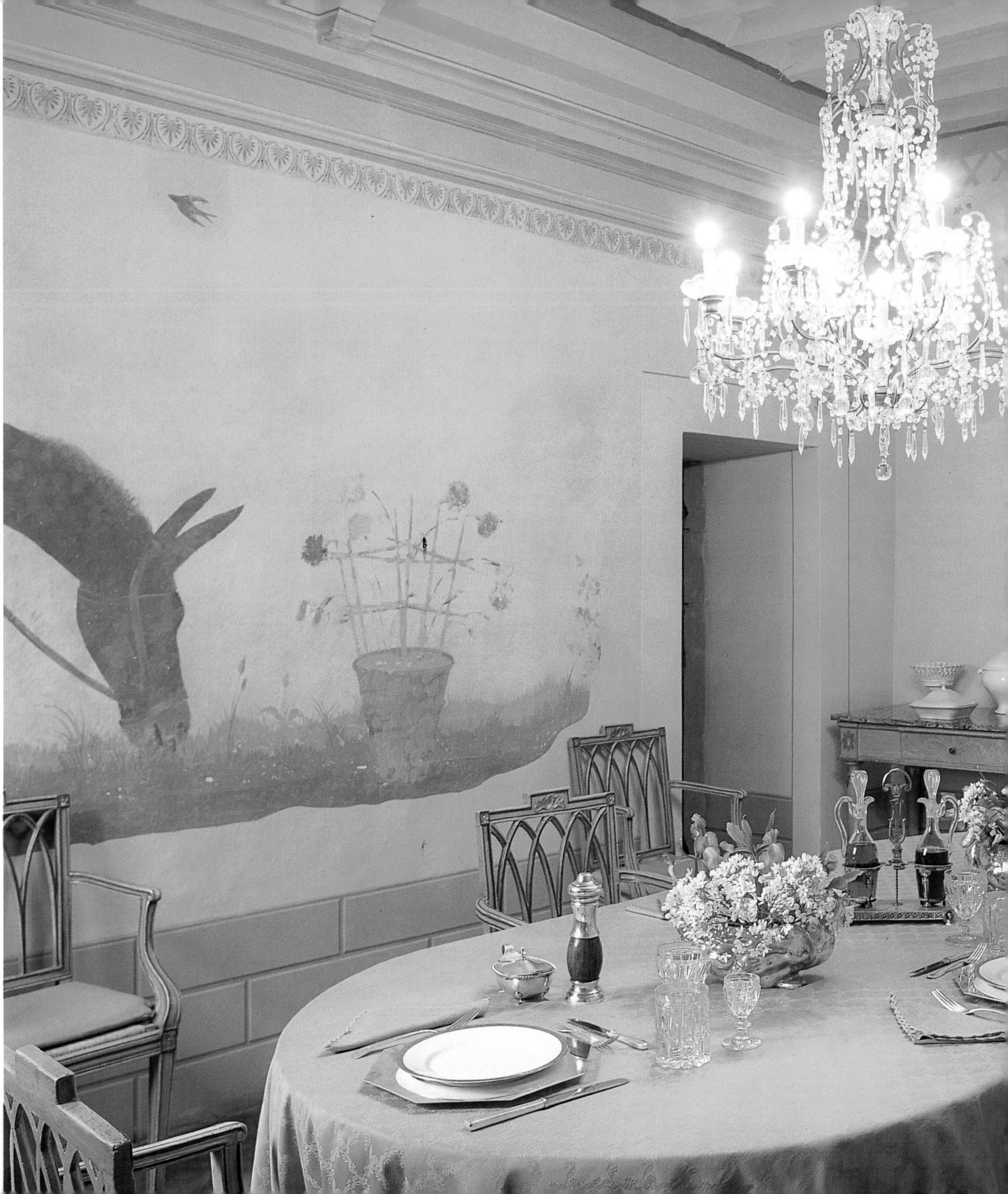

LEFT & BELOW *The naive frescoes in the dining room are among the oldest in the villa. Peeling back centuries of paint, the current owners lovingly restored the rustic scene to it original splendour. The farmyard animals and sunny colours make a charming counterpoint to the elaborate chandelier and elegant dining chairs.*

OPPOSITE & ABOVE

Despite the grandeur and visual richness of the villa, the owner's personal spaces have been arranged to create a cosy and inviting atmosphere. The master bedroom boasts clean lines and minimal decoration, in contrast to the rest of the house. A rug, chaise longue and curtained bed are among the few touches of colour and pattern. The room's character is dictated by the mementoes and personal possessions of the owner. A family portrait hangs over the mantelpiece, while a library wraps itself around two walls. Likewise the study is intended as a private retreat, with elegant but comfortable furnishings. The view takes in the surrounding garden and cultivated fields.

ABOVE & OPPOSITE *The entrance hall of the Castello is the result of a nineteenth-century transformation. The carved stone balustrade, with Ionic capitals, follows the staircase up to the first floor. Ancestral portraits, walking canes kept in a terra-cotta urn and ceremonial spears are all mementoes of the family's past.*

GOTHIC FORTRESS

THE CHIANTI REGION IS RENOWNED FOR PRODUCING TUSCANY'S BEST WINES. IT IS EQUALLY FAMED FOR ITS UNDULATING LAND-SCAPE OF HILL TOWNS, GOLDEN VINEYARDS AND VAST HORIZONS.

Between deep green forests of oak, pine and chestnut trees, meticulously tended rows of vines and silvery stands of olive trees, the occasional castle, hill town or villa comes into view. No longer needed to guard one of the most important routes in Tuscany, these sites are now more valuable for their spectacular views.

Atop a hill overlooking over the Arbia valley, the Castello Brolio is located in the heart of the Chianti region, midway between Florence and Siena. It was in fact this strategic position between the two warring city-states that gave the fortress its complicated history.

During the Middle Ages ownership of the castle bounced back and forth between the two cities. Yet since the eleventh century, despite the vagaries of war, it has remained in the possession of the Ricasoli family, whose descendants still live there.

Through the vicissitudes of history, the structure of the castle has been adapted and enlarged. After an attack in 1478, when the entire building was levelled to the ground, it was rebuilt in 1484, this time by the Florentines. Bastions were erected, great walls of stone and brick, the first of their kind in Italy. Ingeniously designed – probably by the young Renaissance architect Giuliano da Sangallo, who was well known

ABOVE *A neo-gothic window, framed by autumn vines, was added in the nineteenth century when the house was remodelled.*

OPPOSITE *Another result of renovation, the main salon is a neo-gothic extravaganza. Rich furnishings, maiolica and porcelain objects, and a large antique rug all add to the dramatic effect. But by far the most important decorative element is the hand-worked leather that covers the walls.*

for his mastery of fortifications – they have withstood the test of time and stand today as some of the earliest remnants of the structure.

The next big building campaign was carried out four centuries later, in the mid-nineteenth century. The castle was then owned by Bettino Ricasoli, one of united Italy's first prime ministers and known as the Iron Baron. He called in architect Pietro Marchetti to refashion this rough fortress into a sumptuous villa in neo-gothic style. The magnificent crenellated tower, which today overlooks the valley, is the result of this extensive redesign.

Many of the grand rooms inside the Castello bear the mark of this neo-gothic intervention. The grand salon and dining room are furnished with heavily carved wooden tables, chairs and cabinets, and their vast walls glisten under coverings of gilded Spanish leather. Displayed throughout the fortress are the collections of antique paintings, tapestries and ceramics that bear witness to the uninterrupted presence of the Ricasoli family here over the centuries.

The family has maintained an enormous winery since the middle of the last century, when the Baron Ricasoli developed the rules for producing Chianti. Thanks to his early work, the wine now has a guaranteed controlled designation of origin, *Denominazione di Origine Controllata e Garantita* (a mark that singles out wines of unmistakably high quality), and the family's vineyards are part of the elite central region known as Chianti Classico. Down below the Castello, the winery produces over ten million bottles of wine a year under its two labels 'Brolio' (a wine of high quality) and 'Ricasoli' (a wine of medium high quality). With over twenty-five hectares of producing vines, the Ricasoli family is the region's biggest producer of Chianti.

LEFT *Sixteenth-century walls still form a protective ring around the castle. The romantic crenellations were added three centuries later. The vineyards surrounding the castle were the inspiration for former owner Baron Ricasoli's development of the distinctive Chianti blend.*

BELOW *A small Italian-style formal garden was laid out during the nineteenth century. But the rest of the grounds is given over to shady trees and a profusion of native shrubs and wild herbs.*

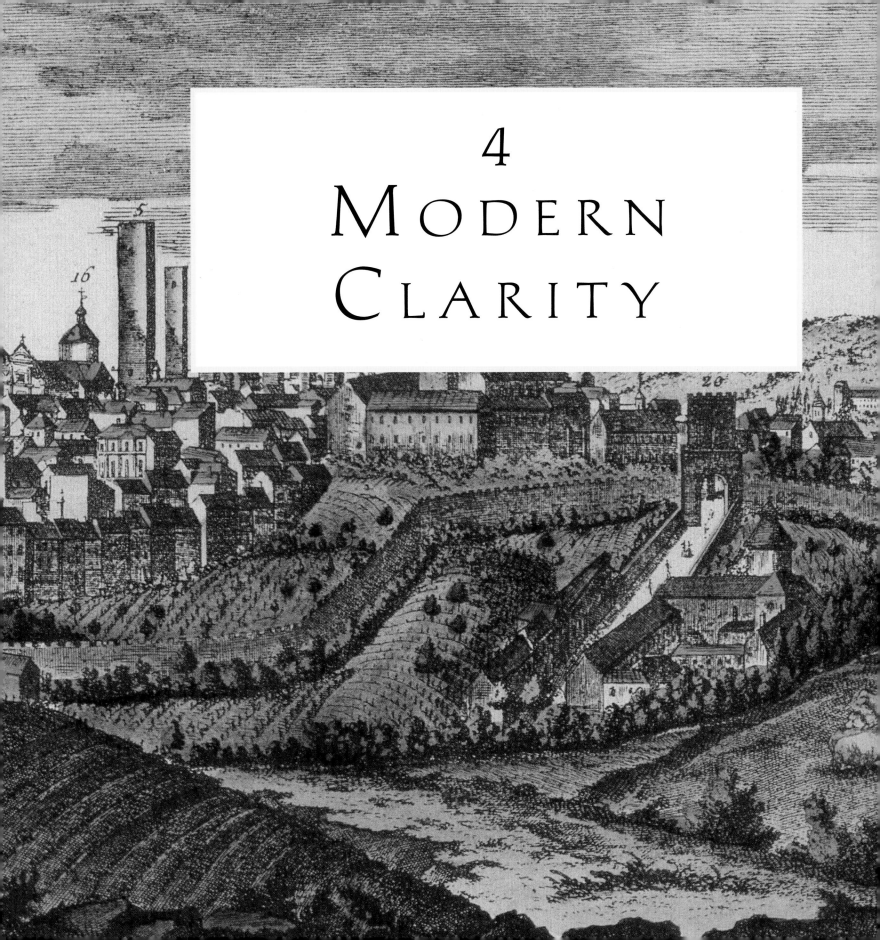

4
MODERN
CLARITY

ABOVE & OPPOSITE *Clean lines and clear colours define the house of Francesco Miani d'Angoris, from the simple bench in a guest bedroom to the architecture itself. Large French doors open out from the living room to a terrace and pool with a very modern look. In place of the usual terra-cotta tones, d'Angoris opted for cool greys.*

NOVEL VARIATIONS

RESTORING ABANDONED TUSCAN HOUSES, HOWEVER ROMANTIC THE IDEA, IS NOT FOR THE FAINT OF HEART, AND THE ROAD TO THE PERFECT FARMHOUSE IS USUALLY A VERY LONG AND BUMPY ONE.

Francesco Miani d'Angoris knows this path well, having restored more than a dozen such houses over the last twenty years in this corner of Tuscany. Where major structural work is required, endless bureaucratic entanglements can make the job even more complicated. But his latest, and most difficult, challenge was not restoring a ruin back to an authentic rustic domain, but building a brand-new house.

What attracted d'Angoris to this parcel of fifty hectares were the magnificent views out over unspoiled countryside. Surrounded by oak forest and pastures, the property was isolated and wild. The sale also included approved plans to build a home, but this meant that d'Angoris was largely bound to the basic design the previous owner had drawn up.

So now the challenge was how to render a new house as charming and rusticated as the abandoned farmhouses he was used to restoring. The rigorous use of old building materials, including aged beams and antique terra-cotta tiles, provided the framework. Careful application of glowing colours and rich textures did the rest, along with family heirlooms which have created a warm, history-laden feeling.

The house is intended as the interior designer's main home, and its layout reflects his twin passions: cooking and entertaining. The large

THIS PAGE & OPPOSITE *The pool area, with its views across to nearby Mount Cetona, is the constant focus of summer living. A nineteenth-century farmhouse table provides the setting for alfresco meals.*

living room stretches the length of the ground floor and provides comfortable seating areas in front of the fireplace or French windows.

Mirroring d'Angoris's casual style, the dining room masquerades as a book-lined study. Nothing formal declares this room's function. Two nineteenth-century pasta tables appear more like library desks, each with its own central lamp, tempting one to pull a book down and start reading. A pair of trophy birds in flight on the wall echoes a decorative element that begins above the main entrance to the house with a bison skull, complete with antlers. Boars heads, antlers and various other paraphernalia give the feeling of an old hunting lodge, emphasized by the location in a wild forest.

Despite the cosy mood of the interior, at the first sign of warm weather, life shifts outdoors. Here the pergola and swimming pool deck come into their own. A long farmhouse table and bench provide the perfect setting for alfresco meals. Reproduction Indian camp beds, laden with cushions, stretch invitingly by the poolside and are perfect for siestas on hot Tuscan summer days.

RIGHT *The positioning of objects in the lounge room is strictly symmetrical, creating a sense of space. However, the flagstone flooring, bright red furnishing fabric and the blackened fireplace all bring a relaxed and cosy feel to the room.*

BELOW *A Japanese kimono stand acts as a coat rack in the entrance hall. Beside it, an antique terra-cotta urn holds a collection of walking sticks.*

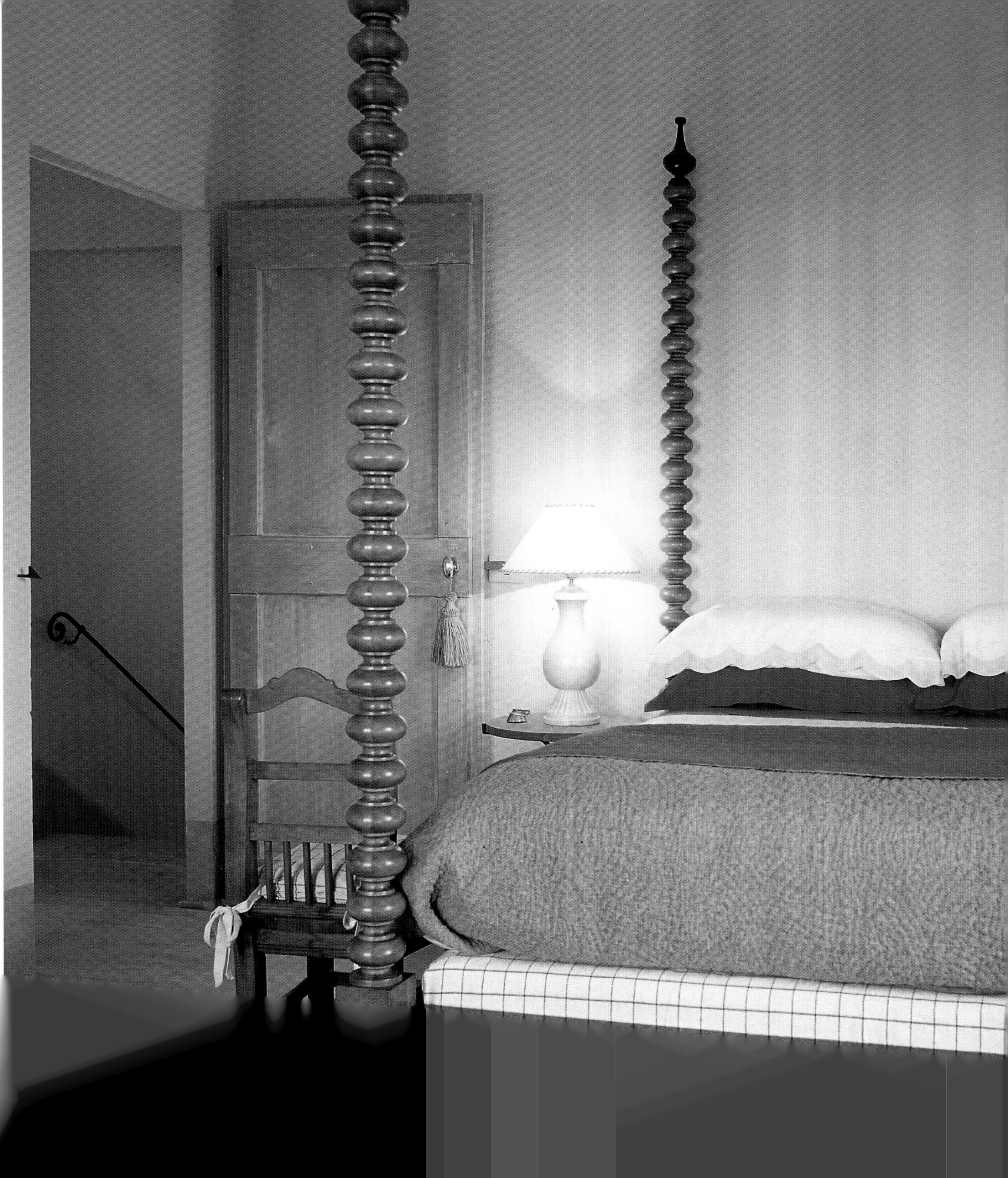

The four-poster bed in the guest bedroom is designed by d'Angoris in a hybrid style he refers to as 'Spanish Inquisition meets American colonial'. A portrait of the designer's great-grandfather hangs above an antique chest of drawers.

LEFT & BELOW *The book-lined dining room feels more like a library. Separate dining tables mimic the reading desks of a library with their individual reading lamps, designed by furniture maker Ilaria Miani. D'Angoris prefers to have two dining tables for dinner parties, as the smaller groupings lend a more intimate feel - so too does the multitude of flickering candles.*

ABOVE & OPPOSITE *In stark contrast to the dark cellars below ground, the living areas of the Castellini house are awash with zinging colours. The corridor that runs the length of the upper floor is painted in warm yellows. All the rooms lead off the corridor, including the violet-blue study just visible.*

RESTORATION PERFECTION

WELL-KNOWN MILAN-BASED INTERIOR DESIGNER PIERO CASTELLINI WAS LOOKING FOR A COUNTRY HOME LARGE ENOUGH TO PROVIDE A COMFORTABLE RETREAT FOR HIS ENTIRE FAMILY TO ENJOY ON HOLIDAY.

The farmhouse he found in the Tuscan hills just south of Siena fitted the bill. When he first discovered Le Fontanelle he immediately saw the potential of the dilapidated farmhouse. His first decision was to strip the house down to its bare fabric, revealing ancient stone, beams and brick. Yet this was not to be a typical restoration, with emphasis on rustic and humble origins. Instead, Castellini took as his starting point the strong voice of the surrounding countryside, intent on capturing the same rugged texture and intensity of the colours visible outside.

The decoration of the house very much reflects the designer's own taste, and pays homage to his personal brand of sophisticated eclecticism. No rough farm tables here. In their place, exquisite examples from various periods intermingle: Louis XVI, Chinese colonial, and neoclassical statuary all have their place.

The most unique aspect of the house is the use of colour. For help in capturing the look and feel of the Tuscan palette, he turned to artist Adam Alvarez, a Briton transplanted to Chianti. Using only natural pigments, he created almost transparent layers of colour that suffuse the rooms as the light pours through the windows. The ground floor is dominated by warm tones of ochre and yellow, while the upper floor gives

ABOVE, RIGHT & OPPOSITE

Blue-green shutters and doors punch through the golden hues of the exterior stucco, while climbing roses soften the austere lines of the house. Further devices to prettify the otherwise plain facade include hand-thrown terra-cotta urns planted with geraniums and wide blue-and-white stripes decorating an alcove off the courtyard.

way to a cooler range of violets and blues.

Bathrooms as well are given the full Castellini treatment. Rather than have each one different, he chose the pleasing palette of ivory and terra-cotta, played out in differing patterns, in each room. Alvarez applied his magic on the walls, while the floors were laid out in a checkerboard pattern of unwaxed matt tiles.

Castellini is known for his attention to detail, and every object in his own house reflects this approach. The quality of the bedlinen or the types of herbs in the garden are as important to him as the beams that support the roof or the size of the windows that break the facade. All work together harmoniously. A recurring theme throughout the house is Castellini's passion for beautiful fabrics. Indian cotton saris float from a four poster bed in one room, while formal toile-de-Jouys are used in another. Although textures and prints change from room to room, they are united by the designer's personal vision.

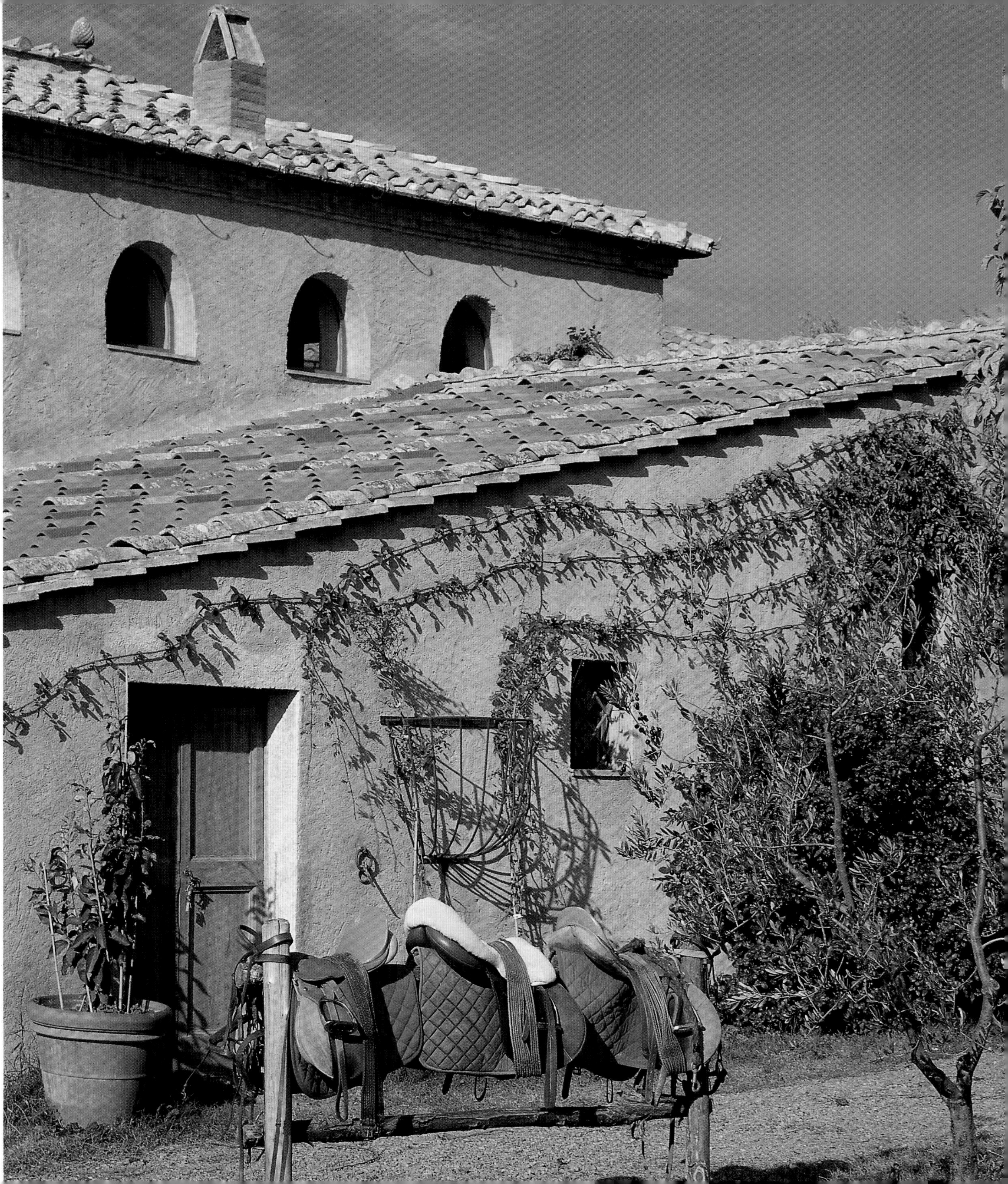

*Much of daily life
at the house revolves
around Piero
Castellini's stable of
horses. Saddles stand
ready outside the
stables for a mid-
morning ride. A pair
of riding boots sits
waiting at the entrance
to the house. The Louis
XVI sofa is covered in
a Pierre Frey fabric.*

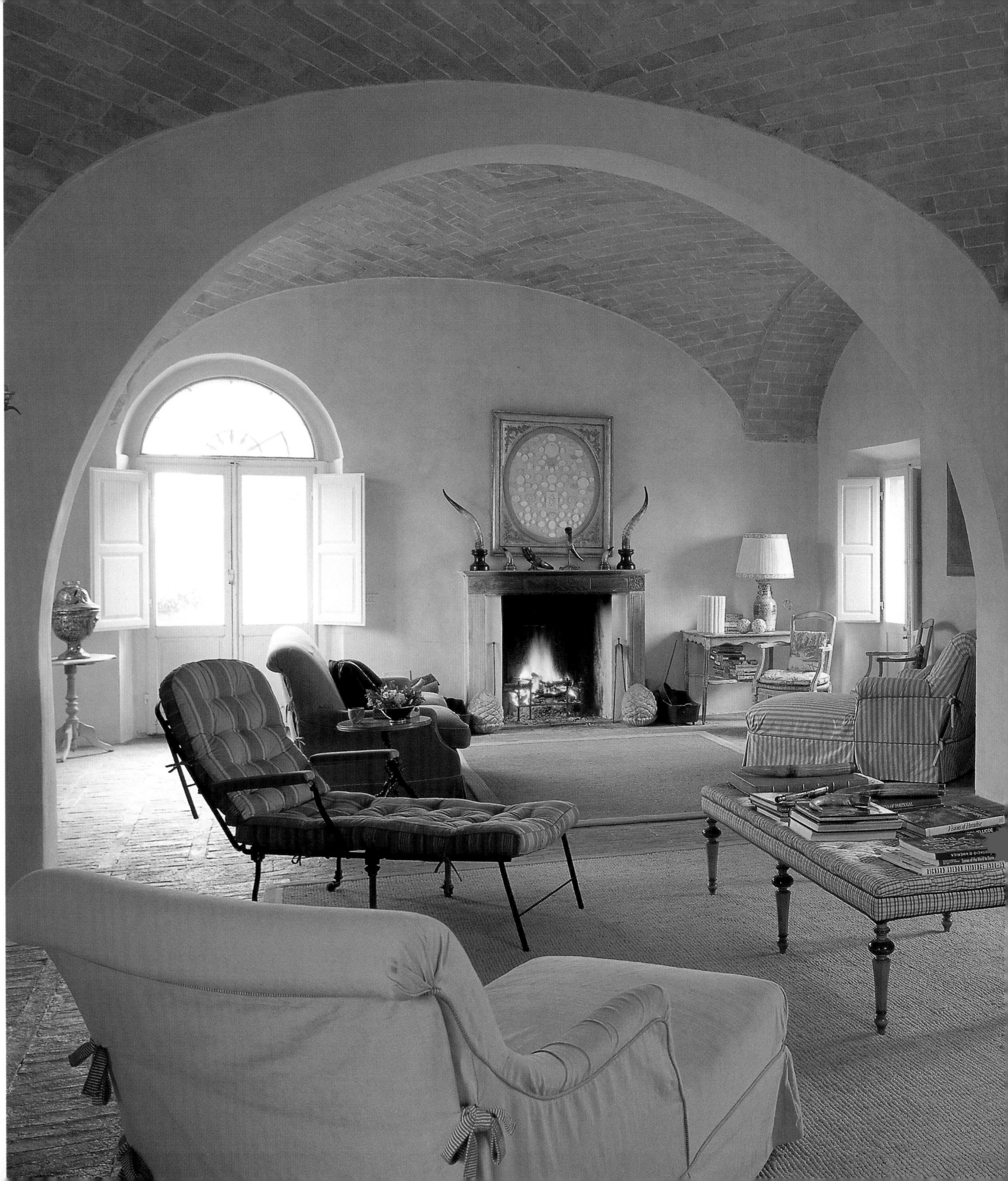

LEFT & BELOW *The soaring arches that frame the main living room are an original part of this suite of ground-floor rooms. Shades of orange and ochre enfold the spacious room, the seemingly perfect colour composition broken only by the blackened surround of the fireplace. Above the mantelpiece, a collection of miniature eighteenth-century plaster portraits is enclosed in a frame.*

OPPOSITE & ABOVE

An adjoining kitchen and dining area provides a focus for meal times. The warm yellow walls, terra-cotta floors and abundance of natural light make this one of the most inviting parts of the house. In the kitchen, an iron crockery stand displays a collection of antique plates. A faux bamboo cupboard from the nineteenth century provides extra storage space. The dining room is given over to a large cherry-wood table and a selection of eighteenth- and nineteenth-century lacquered chairs. Local cheeses, salami, prosciutto and bread provide an impromptu lunch, accompanied by red wine bought from the cantina next door and decanted into a carafe.

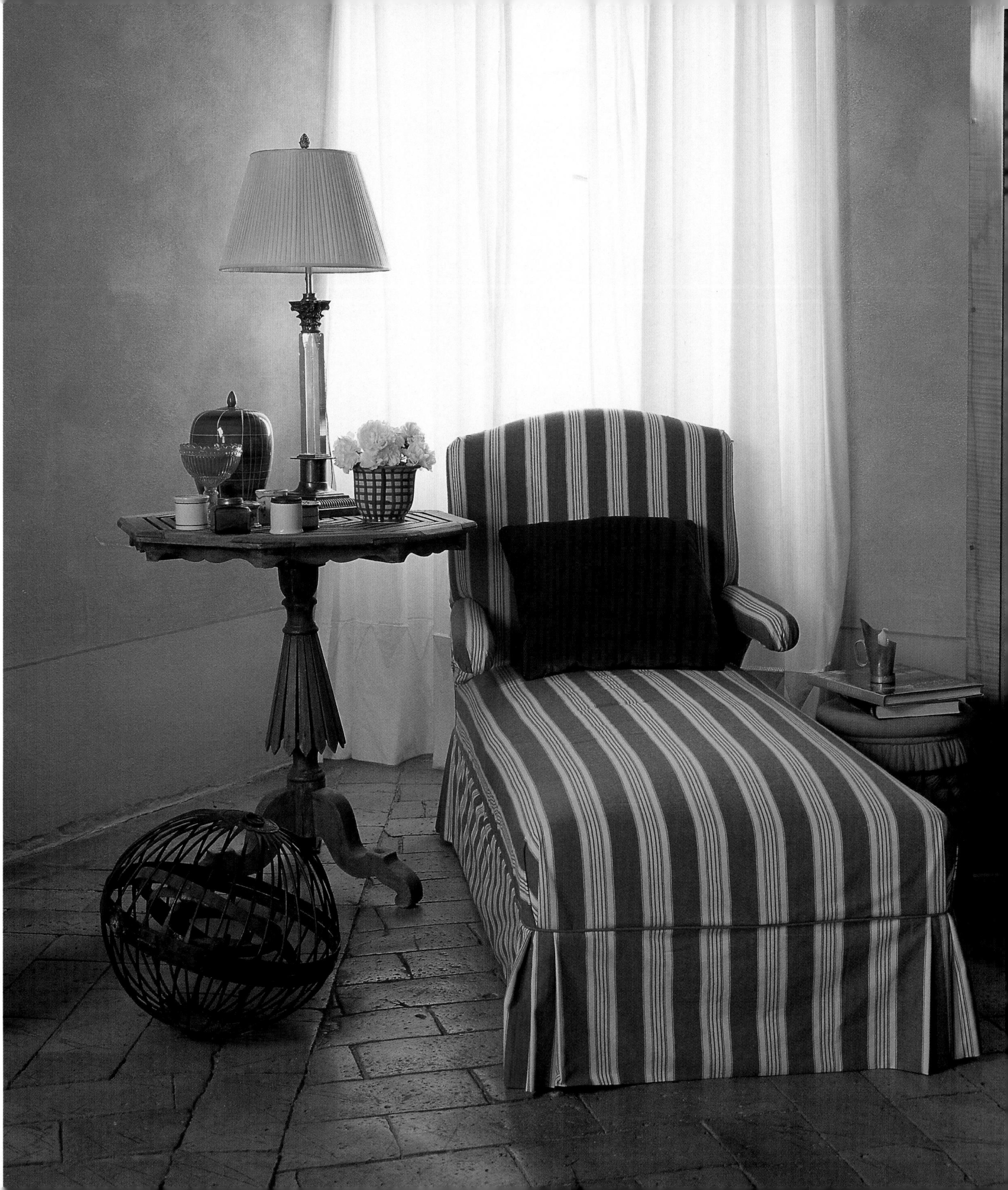

OPPOSITE, LEFT & BELOW *The study adjoins the master bedroom and provides a space for Castellini to read and work on his architectural projects. A hand-tinted paint washes the room in a calming sea of blue, echoed in the ticking covering the day bed. The mantelpiece supports a collection of blue porcelain; an eighteenth-century Piedmontese cameo hangs above. Original terra-cotta flooring and exposed beams lend the room a warm rustic quality.*

ABOVE & OPPOSITE *The sober lines of Tenuta di Trinoro are reflected in a shallow manmade pond. The collection of buildings includes a medieval tower, its entrance marked by a vivid cupola. The brightly coloured folly was added by the owner, Andrea Franchetti, and pays homage to the days of the Crusades, when the original watchtower was always manned.*

CURRENT VINTAGE

IT IS APPROPRIATE THAT TENUTA DI TRINORO IS THE NAME OF BOTH THE ROBUST RED WINE THAT ITALIAN VINTNER ANDREA FRANCHETTI PRODUCES, AND THE TUSCAN HOME OVERLOOKING HIS VINEYARDS.

One led to the other and they are part of the complicated story that brought him, and keeps him, in southern Tuscany. Franchetti knew the area well, visiting the homes of friends and family since he was a child. In 1981 he finally bought himself a cluster of old farmhouses, all sadly neglected and half collapsed. Restoring first one and then another, he found himself slipping slowly into the country way of life, further and further away from his career as a wine distributor in New York.

How to remain in the area, supporting his passion for restoring old houses, as well as continuing to use his experience in the field of wine? In 1990 he planted the first vines on his property, intent on producing a big, full-bodied red wine. The fruits of his labour were harvested in 1995 and are now on the market under his label 'Tenuta di Trinoro'. While the area has no great wine-growing tradition comparable to that of nearby Montalcino, all Italian appellations are a relatively new occurrence and Franchetti is just one of a growing number of enthusiasts intent on producing new and important wines.

Franchetti's home, which is really a collection of several buildings, overlooks the Val d'Orcia, a magical valley that lies along the southern border of Tuscany. Views from the upper windows take in the vast

ABOVE *Empty wine casks are stacked in the shade, waiting to be cleaned and refilled with the fruit of the year's harvest.*

OPPOSITE *The furnishing in Franchetti's house is kept to a minimum. Many of the pieces were bought locally and stripped back to reveal their original patinas.*

sweep of northern Tuscany. The days of border controls are long past, but the medieval tower which forms the nucleus of one of the houses is testament to the precarious position of these outposts. Perched atop the ridge, these series of towers could pass messages from one to the next, all the way back to Florence.

Franchetti's life is divided between his houses. Sleeping in one, he may decide to breakfast in another and then go back to the first for a mid-afternoon siesta. The interiors reflect this casual outlook and are a mixture of textures and colours that reflect his personal taste.

As far as possible during the restoration, materials were left as they were found. The top level of one of the buildings was in such good shape that the entire original floor, constructed out of handmade terra-cotta tiles, was retained, needing only a clean-up and a coat of wax. While most of the roofing had to be patched up, old tiles from the area were used to retain the original effect. One exception is the hot pink cupola which tops a doorway. This was Franchetti's addition and its Eastern feeling pays poetic homage to the days of the Crusades, when the watchtower was always manned.

The ogive arches over some of the doors are original thirteenth-century architectural elements. Newer additions are the stretches of exterior paving constructed from river stones. While not a typical Tuscan element, the technique does date back to the Middle Ages, and is often found in fortifications throughout Europe. Although Franchetti chose this method for its beauty, it is extremely durable as well, since the stones are sunk to three quarters of their depth into the earth. They will stay in place for decades to come, providing a sound surface over which barrels of wine will clatter on their way to the cellars.

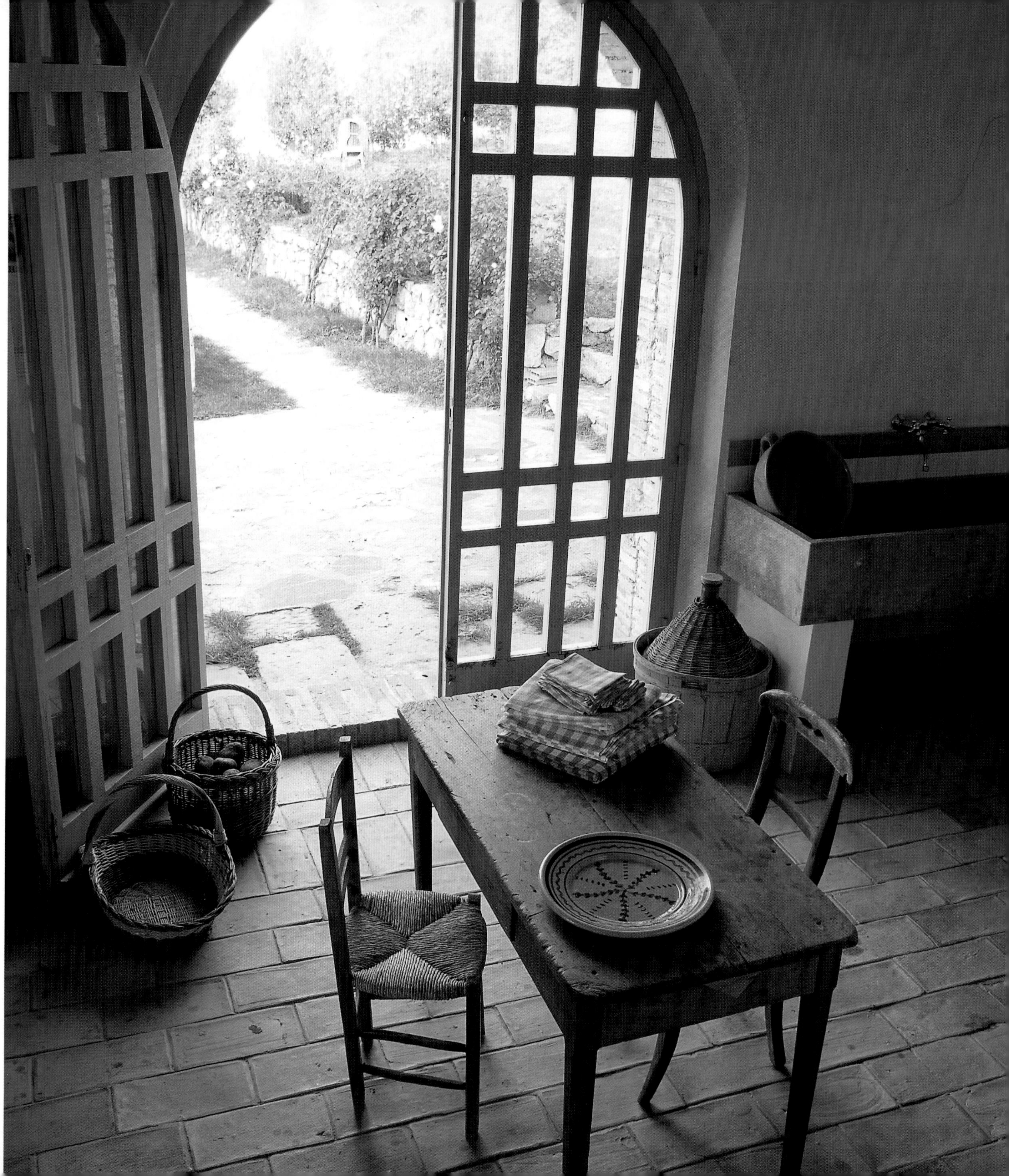

OPPOSITE *The ground floor, as in all Tuscan country homes, was originally used as an animal stall. Sunlight illuminates what now serves as a spacious kitchen.*

LEFT *Vineyards march across the valley. Cabernet Franc, Cabernet Sauvignon and Merlot varieties are blended with Petit Verdot and a mixture of Italian grapes to produce Franchetti's wine.*

BELOW, LEFT & RIGHT *Details of life at Tenuta di Trinoro: the cellar entrance; and staples of robust Tuscan cooking.*

NATURAL SELECTION

ABOVE & OPPOSITE *Wood-burning fireplaces heat the house during the winter months, using wood cut from nearby forests. In the ground-floor sitting room, the shape of the chimney flue protrudes above a massive stone mantelpiece. In contrast to its heavy lines, a light, leafy frieze encircles the room just below the beamed ceiling.*

WHILE WALKING ONE CRISP AUTUMN DAY, AS THE LEAVES WERE BEGINNING TO TURN, GIORGIO AND GAIA FRANCHETTI SPOTTED THEIR NEXT PROJECT, A REMOTE AND ABANDONED FARMHOUSE.

The couple had just finished restoring a farmhouse in Val d'Orcia and were enjoying one of the reasons they have settled in the area: the amazing landscape. Gaia, looking off across the valley towards a wild, uninhabited section of the hillside, thought she spotted a house in the forest. Giorgio, who prides himself on an intimate knowledge of every square inch of this corner of Tuscany, said it was impossible. A bet between husband and wife left Gaia the winner and the couple the owner of yet another house in desperate need of attention.

After a few hours of exploration and research, the couple found the house, located the owners and made 'I Troscioni' their own. It is almost impossible to find abandoned houses these days in Tuscany, and the couple couldn't believe their luck. I Troscioni sits on a peaceful plain, perched high above the Val d'Orcia. Views stretch out for miles and embrace the wild side of the valley. In fact they have no nearby neighbours, save wild boar and the occasional fox.

Three years of restoration work began with Giorgio's construction of a 'ruined' tower. The only way to gain permission from the stringent planning commission for the construction of a tower was to convince them that there was already one there. The foundation was laid and two

storeys of fortifications erected, with suitably crumbled edges at the top: an instant medieval ruin. The planning commission then granted the rights to restore the structure to its 'original' height of four storeys.

Since this was the second country house that Gaia had worked on she knew exactly how she wanted it to look. Instead of the pristine white used for most farmhouse conversions, she opted for coloured interior walls. Rooms are painted in the local style, with the colour applied almost all the way up the wall, then topped by a thin band of a contrasting tone.

Colour also plays an important role in the choice of furniture. The Franchettis have been collecting painted furniture from the Alto Adige region of northern Italy for years, beginning when these now-rare pieces were still comparatively easy to find. Simple, massive forms are treated with a delicateness of both shade and design. Often the original painted decoration of two hundred years ago will have been painted over, with the later coats of paint perfectly preserving the patina underneath, waiting to be restored.

Another motif that runs throughout the house is Gaia's interest in all things Indian. Many of the fabrics she uses are from the textile collection she produces, the 'Indo Roman Collection'. Combining Indian fabrics with antique Roman and Indian designs and symbols, Gaia produces curtains, bedspreads, table cloths and towels. Texture, too, plays an important role. All of the Indian fabrics are handloomed, as they have been for hundreds of years, conveying a sense of history not found in industrially produced textiles. And so textures and colours are interwoven: smooth terra-cotta tiles, nubbly hot orange bedspreads, diaphanous curtain of muslin and the rough-hewn stones of the exterior. All work together to produce something completely different, a modern presence in the timeless setting of Tuscany.

ABOVE & OPPOSITE *Textures and colours drawn from nature dominate the house, whether in the doors of a large armadio, or wardrobe, from northern Italy or the warm, sunlit tones of the living room, with its curtains crafted from Indian saris.*

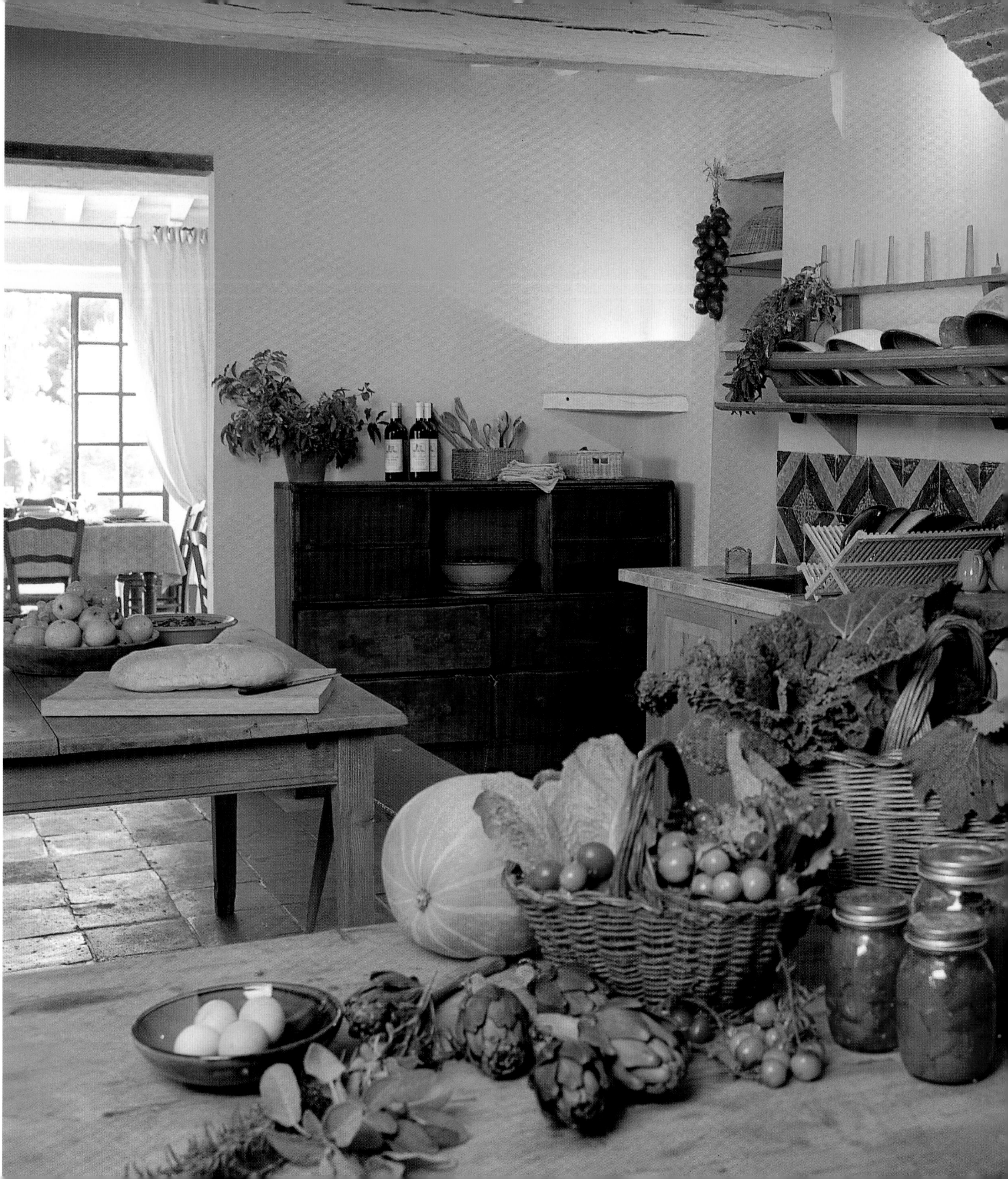

LEFT & BELOW *The expansive kitchen and adjoining dining room take up a good portion of the ground floor. The kitchen is the focus of household life at most times of the year but is a hive of activity during August, when tomatoes from the vegetable garden are preserved in jars.*

ABOVE & OPPOSITE *A pared-down rusticity is the key to Vibeke Lökkeberg's tranquil house. In one of the guest bathrooms, a basket of dried lavender from the garden, an antique mirror and a single candle create a soothing atmosphere. Equally calming is the guest kitchen, with solid country furniture washed in green and scrubbed back to reveal the timber patina.*

INSPIRED SOLITUDE

SOME PEOPLE SEEK THE TRANQUIL COUNTRY LIFE OF TUSCANY TO ESCAPE FROM WORK. OTHERS ARE ATTRACTED BY THE TEXTURES AND TASTES THAT THE AREA OFFERS UP TO ALL WHO CARE TO LINGER.

Vibeke Lökkeberg came to this corner of Tuscany to capture all this and more. For in restoring Il Casone, she has created something unique: a retreat tucked away in the Tuscan hills, where she comes to relax, certainly, but also to find the peace and silence necessary for creativity.

Lökkeberg is a Norwegian film director who writes and stars in her own films. While on holiday here ten years ago, she came across this large, rambling, run-down house and decided to sink her roots in this sunny clime, far from home. The house was quite large and most of it was built in the last century. Although much loved, Il Casone resisted her attentions, and she wasn't quite satisfied with the solutions she had come up with for transforming the ramshackle building. Luckily, neighbours Michele Cantatore (an architect) and Emanuela Stramana (an interior designer) were willing and able to help her rework this farmhouse into a sober, yet warmly elegant, rural hideaway.

When not in residence, Lökkeberg often lends the house to friends and colleagues, writers and artists looking for a little solitude and the time to create. The ingenious layout of the house allows a great deal of privacy for both guests and owners. Four independent suites, complete with kitchens, allow visitors to spend whole days without seeing

OPPOSITE & BELOW *Although the house is undeniably rustic in its architectural detail and its building materials, Lökkeberg has endowed it with a modern edge by streamlining the decoration, using simple, robust furnishings, and by keeping the rooms purposefully minimal. In the guest bedroom, the twin beds are given a sophisticated yet pure look with white cotton canopies. The dining room features a solid chestnut table with a marble top.*

another soul. A spacious living room and outdoor terraces provide opportunities to socialize for those who are willing.

Warm yellows and ochres were used for the interior walls throughout the house. Applied unevenly, these earth tones provide a textured background for the austere lines of rustic furnishings or for canopied beds draped in stiff folds of white linen. Another constant element is the use of handmade terra-cotta tiles on the floors, broken only by the occasional throw rug. The impression is of uncluttered modernity and provincial comfort, a merging of Tuscan warmth and Scandinavian purity.

The garden surrounding the building has been kept simple. A few oaks provide shade, a handful of rosemary bushes scent the air and scented roses burst into bloom each May. Together, house and garden provide a soothing and unpretentious environment for all those who come to Il Casone to rest, work and find inspiration.

Vibeke Lökkeberg's
Scandinavian roots
are clearly evident in
the bathroom, with its
scrubbed, wholesome
looks and earthy
romance.

LEFT
Large-brimmed
straw hats stand ready
for guests who venture
out into the bright
Tuscan sunshine.

LEFT & BELOW *The master suite, with its canopied bed, drapes and chair covers in bleached desert colours, is as sumptuous as Lökkeberg's spare aesthetic allows. The canopies were designed by her neighbour Emanuela Stramana and give the room a Middle Eastern feel. Other furnishings include a chaise longue covered in deep green velvet and a pair of Oriental rugs, which provide a contrast to the pale walls and drapes.*

LIVING IN TUSCANY

TUSCANY IS A RICH TAPESTRY OF THE SENSES. WITHIN ITS BORDERS THIS ITALIAN PROVINCE OFFERS A SEEMINGLY LIMITLESS NUMBER OF GEOGRAPHICAL, CULTURAL AND CULINARY EXPERIENCES, MAKING IT ONE OF THE MOST SUMPTUOUS PLACES TO LIVE IN THE WORLD. SOME ARE DRAWN BY ITS MATCHLESS RENAISSANCE ARCHITECTURE, OTHERS BY THE SENSUOUS FLAVOURS OF THE SEASONAL FOOD, OR BY ITS WHITE BEACHES, FIELDS OF SUNFLOWERS OR SNOW-CAPPED MOUNTAINS. THE CONTINUAL PULL OF TUSCANY IS DUE TO ALL OF THESE THINGS AND MORE.

WINE & PRODUCE

CANTINA COOPERATIVA MORELLINO

Scansano

Località Saragiolo (Grosseto)

tel 0564-507288

ENOTECA DEL CHIANTI CLASSICO GALLO NERO

Piazzetta Santa Croce 8,

Florence

tel 055-853297

Stocks the most important wines in the Chianti region.

CANTINE BARONCINI

San Gimignano (Siena)

tel 0577-940600

Wine tastings of the local Vernaccia.

FATTORIA DEI BARBI

Montalcino

Località Podernovi (Siena)

tel 0577-848277

LA BOTTEGA DEL VINO

Via della Rocca 13

Castellina in Chianti (Siena)

tel 0577-741110

FRANTOIO SANMINIATESE

Via Maremmana 8

Località La Serra (Pisa)

Specializes in olive oil.

FATTORIA COLLEVERDE MATRAIA

Località Matraia (Lucca)

tel 0583-402310 fax 0583-402313

Farm specializing in Lucca olive oils.

FATTORIA DI FORCI

Località Forci (Lucca)

tel 0583-349007

Farm selling olive oil, wine and honey.

CASEIFICIO CUGUSI

Via di Gracciano nel Corso 31

Montepulciano (Siena)

tel 0578-757558 fax 0578-758748

Excellent selection of Pecorino cheeses.

AGRICOLA LA PARRINA

Via Aurelia at km 146

Orbetello (Grosseto)

tel 0564-862636

For homemade Pecorino cheese.

DINING

• *For Provincial Specialties:*

LA CANTINA DI CARIGNANO
Via per Sant 'Alessio 3618
Carignano (Lucca)
tel 0583-329618

LA CECEA
Commune di Capanori
Località Coselli
(Lucca)
tel 0583-94130

PUCCINI
Corte San Lorenzo 1
Lucca
tel 0583-316116

DA CECCO
Via Forti 96, Pescia
(Pistoia)
tel 0572-477955

LA MORA
Via Sesto 1748
Ponte a Moriano
(Lucca)
tel 0583-406402

LA TENDA ROSSA
Piazza del Monumento 9
Località Cerbaia (Florence)
tel 055-826132

ARNOLFO
Via XX Septembre 50-52-A
Colle Val d'Elsa (Siena)
tel 0577-920549

LOCANDA DELL'AMOROSA
2km south of Sinalunga
(Siena)
tel 0577-679497

• *For Seafood Specialties:*

GAMBERO ROSSO
Piazza della Vittoria 13
San Vincenzo (Livorno)
tel 0565-701021

• *For Florentine Meat Dishes:*

TAVERNA DEL CHIANTI
Via del Sergente 5
Vagliagli, Castellina in Chianti
(Siena)
tel 0577-322532

LA TORRE
Piazza del Comune 17
Castellina in Chianti (Siena)
tel 0577-740236

• *For Soups:*

LOCANDA LAUDOMIA
Via Case Ciani 1
Poderi di Montemerano
Manciano (Grosseto)
tel 0564-620062

LA TAVERNA DEI BARBI
Podernovi, Montalcino (Siena)
tel 0577-849357

BUCA DI SANT' ANTONIO
Via della Cervia 3, Lucca
tel 0583-55881

• *For Atmosphere:*

RELAIS LA SUVERA
Via della Suvera, Pievescola
Casole d'Elsa (Siena)
tel 0577-960300

LA GRIGLIA
Via San Matteo 34
San Gimignano (Siena)
tel 0577-940005

HOTELS & HOUSES

• *Exclusive Hotels*

HOTEL VILLA LA PRINCIPESSA
Via della Chiesa 462
Massa Pisana (Lucca)
tel 0583-935355 fax 0583-379136
Eighteenth-century residence.

IL PELLICANO
Strada Panoramica
Porto Ercole (Grosseto)
tel 0564-833801 fax 0564-833418
Luxury cottages and private beach.

LA CERTOSA DI MAGGIANO
Strada di Certosa 82
Maggiano (Siena)
tel 0577-288180

LA SUVERA
Pivescola (Siena)
tel 0577-960300 fax 0577-960220

CASTELLO DI SPALTENNA
Gaiole in Chianti (Siena)
tel 0577-749483 fax 0577-749269

LOCANDA L'ELISA
Via Nuova per Pisa 1952 (Lucca)
tel 0583-379737 fax 0583-379019

• *Boutique Hotels*

VILLA VILLORESI
Via Ciampi 6, Sesto Fiorentino (Florence)
tel 055-443212/443692 fax 055-4489032
Antique villa transformed into a hotel.

IL CHIOSTRO DI PIENZA
Corso Rossellino 26
Pienza (Siena)
tel 0578-748400 fax 0578-748440
Restored convent with pool and valley view.

RELAIS FATTORIA VIGNALE
Via Pianigiani 8
Radda in Chianti (Siena)
tel 0577-738300 fax 0577-738592
In the heart of Chianti.

IL FALCONIERE
Località San Martino 370
Cortona (Arezzo)
tel 0575-612679 fax 0575-612927
Refined villa set in parkland.

RELAIS BORGO SAN FELICE
Località San Felice
Castelnuovo Berardenga (Siena)
tel 0577-359260 fax 0577-359089
*Restored medieval village with
hotel & winery.*

• *Private Homes & Castles*

CASTELLO DI FONTERUTOLI
Frazione di Fonterutoli
Castellina in Chianti (Siena)
tel 0577-740476 fax 0577-741070

MONTE SANTE MARIE
Asciano (Siena)
tel/fax 0577-700020

CASTELLO DI MONTAUTO
Località Montauto
Anghiari (Arezzo)
tel 0575-723004

FATTORIA MAIONCHI
Capannori (Lucca)
tel/fax 0583-978194

GHIACCIO BOSCO
Strada della Sgrilla 4
Capalbio (Grosseto)
tel/fax 0564-896539

IL PORNELLETTO
Via Cassia Aurelia Est 6
Cetona (Siena)
tel/fax 0578-222083

• *Convents & Abbeys*

LA VERNA
Località Chiusi Della Verna (Arezzo)
tel 0575-5341 fax 0575-599320

MONTE OLIVETO MAGGIORE
Località Chiusure (Siena)
tel 0577-707017

• *House & Villa Rental Agencies*

SOLEMAR
Via Cavour 80 (Florence)
tel 055-239361 fax 055-287157

TERRE TOSCANE
Via Tatro 19
Montepulciano (Siena)
tel 0578-758582 fax 0578-757098

SALOGI
Via San Gregorio 5
Lucca
tel 0583-48717 fax 0583-48727

GARDENS

VILLA REALE DI MARLIA

Via Fraga Alta, Marlia (Lucca)
tel 0583-30108
*Hours: 10–11; 15–18; guided tours every
hour, from April 1st to November 30th.
Closed on Mondays from December
to April.*

VILLA MANSI

Segromigno in Monte (Lucca)
fax 0583-928114
*Hours: 10–12.30; 14.30–18.
Closed Monday.*

VILLA TORRIGIANI (CAMIGLIANO)

Camigliano (Lucca)
tel 0583-928041
*Hours 10–12; 15–17 until November;
guided tours every 20 min.
Closed Tuesday.*

VILLA GARZONI

Collodi, Pescia (Pistoia)
tel 0572-429590
*Hours: 10–sunset. Closed November 15th
to March 30th.*

VILLA MEDICEA DI CASTELLO

Via di Castello, Castello
Sesto Fiorentino (Florence)
tel 055-454791
*Hours: 9–18.30. Closed 2nd and 3rd
Monday of the month.*

VILLA MEDICEA LA PETRAIA

Via della Petraia 40, Castello
Sesto Fiorentino (Florence)
tel 055-452391
*Hours: 9–18.30. Closed 2nd and 3rd
Monday of the month.*

VILLA BERNARDINI

Via Vercianese 573
Vicopelago (Lucca)
tel 0583-370327
*Hours: By appointment only.
Closed Monday.*

CRAFTS

VALORIANI
Piazza Matteotti 25
Greve, Chianti (Florence)
tel 055-854315
Hand-embroidered linen.

TESSITURE ARTISTICHE LUCCHESI
Villa Gianni, Via dei Gianni 302
S.S. Annunziata (Lucca)
tel 0583-998126 fax 0583-999166
Brightly coloured woven silks.

COLTELLERIE BARTOLINI
Via Roma 43
Scarperia (Florence)
tel 055-846585
Knives with precious wooden handles.

**CONSORZIO CRISTALLO
DI COLLE VAL D'ELSA**
Via di Castello 33
Colle Val d'Elsa (Siena)
tel 0577-924135
*Engraved, handblown crystal vases
and glasses.*

CERAMICHE DEL BORGO
Via XX Settembre, corner of Via Marconi
Montelupo (Florence)
tel 0571-518856
Decorative ceramic plates and vases.

DOLFI
Via Tosco Romagnola 1
Antinoro, Montelupo (Florence)
tel 0571-51264 fax 0571-910116
*Ceramic plates with classical
bird decoration.*

ELSA GROSPIETRO
Via del Cerro 7
Tavarnelle Val di Pesa (Florence)
tel 055-8050106
*Traditional parchment lampshades
with dried flowers.*

THESE & PRECEDING PAGES *Interior glimpses,
gourmet delicacies and classic views of Tuscany.*

Index

Note: references in *italics* are to captions.

ACKNOWLEDGMENTS

The publishers would like to extend sincere thanks to Marchesa Laura Mansi Salom and Isabella Vincenzini
for their invaluable contribution. Thank you also to Mike Spiller at Pentrix Design, Gwynn-fyl Lowe, Jorge de los Rios,
and all those who kindly allowed their homes to be photographed.

ADDITIONAL IMAGES

The four maps above, featured as chapter openers in Private Tuscany, *are reproductions of original
sixteenth-century prints depicting the great Tuscan cities.*